LIVING WILD

Never say die till you're dead!

Lord Robert Baden-Powell, K.C.B.

We are the Pilgrims, master; we shall go
Always a little further: it may be
Beyond that last blue mountain barred with snow,
Across that angry or that glimmering sea

From 'The Golden Journey to Samarkand' by J. E. Flecker,
inscribed on the memorial clock tower at SAS headquarters, Hereford

LIVING WILD

WILD

The Ultimate Guide to Scouting and Fieldcraft

Bear Grylls

Books

This book is dedicated to every one of the 28 million Scouts worldwide. You are part of a global force for good and one of the largest, most positive youth movements of all time. That is good reason to be proud. But Scouting pride requires us then to walk humbly and to give of ourselves. Remember that your strength lies in the skills you are learning, the camaraderie you share and the adventures you are living.

As UK Chief Scout, I am continually filled with admiration for the great spirit that I see in Scouts from all over the world. Long may that spirit thrive.

Bear Grylls, UK Chief Scout

Contents

INTRODUCTION

More than a century ago, a Lieutenant General in the British Army organized a week-long camp for twenty boys on Brownsea Island in the south of England. His name was Robert Baden-Powell. He called his recruits 'scouts', after the military scouts who, in his own words, were 'chosen for [their] cleverness and pluck to go out in front of an army in war to find out where the enemy are'. The skills he taught his scouts were those he himself had mastered during a spectacular military career; skills such as observation, woodcraft, life-saving and shelter building.

Baden-Powell could never have imagined that his Scouting movement would be bigger today than it ever has been. Or maybe he could. But then, 'cleverness and pluck' never go out of fashion, and they are really what this book is all about. Indeed, cleverness and pluck are the beating heart of a Scout.

In the hundred years since Baden-Powell started the Scouting movement, many things have changed. Cities have grown, technology has moved on. But the natural world remains timeless. The stars we use to navigate by are still in the same place; the sun still rises in the east and sets in the west; animals still cast the same tracks and fire still burns just as bright. Our duty as Scouts is to nurture this natural world and every living being in it, to understand the wild, to harness it and to have the courage to follow our God-given spirit of adventure wherever it leads.

I have often written in books about survival or the great outdoors with much reference to previous expeditions or adventures that I have been lucky enough to be involved with. But I have rarely written about the skills I learned during my time with 21 SAS. Much of the information contained in this book comes from these skills that I continue to use to this day. The reason for this is simple. There is a very strong link between the disciplines crucial to the world of Special Forces and those used in the world of Scouting. What I have endeavoured to do in this manual is to highlight those links and adapt many of the practices that make good Special Operations soldiers to the skills required to be an elite pathfinding Scout.

The Scouting motto is 'Be Prepared', and life, in essence, is all about being prepared. Being prepared and trained for adventure, trained to survive, trained to operate in small teams, being prepared to understand nature and how to live wild, and ultimately being prepared for both life and the life-after. It is through our faith that we find peace, but that same faith can also give us great boldness to reach out that little bit further than maybe we are comfortable. Everything worthwhile in life comes from reaching beyond that point of comfort; daring to risk it all; following our dreams despite the cost; loving despite the pain; hoping despite the doubts; and living boldly despite the fear. If I have learned anything it is that together we are stronger. The great key to Scouting and living wild is to embrace that: to laugh, to strive, to dream and to explore, and to take those you love along with you for the ride.

So get out there, guys! Life is an adventure that is best lived boldly.

God bless, and go for it.

Bear.

Lt Cdr *(Hon)* Bear Grylls RN
UK Chief Scout

Chapter 1

GEAR

what the pros use, what you really need and what you don't

'Adventure only happens to those
incompetent of planning an expedition.'

Roald Amundsen, polar explorer

PROTECTION FROM THE WIND, RAIN, COLD, HEAT AND SUN – THE KILLER COMBINATIONS

Don't underestimate the elements. You don't have to be exposed to the heat of the Sahara or the biting chill of Antarctica: the weather can kill you wherever you are. Respect it, understand it: then you have a chance.

To understand how the killer combinations of wind, rain, cold, heat and sun can affect you, you need to understand how your body deals with temperature. Human beings are 'homotherms'. This means that they keep their body temperature at a constant level. Various mechanisms have evolved to let us do this. For example, when we get hot, we sweat – our body's way of cooling us down; when we get cold, we shiver – a reflex action that makes our muscles move and so create warmth by expending energy.

Regulating our temperature like this is essential for survival. Our bodies consist of a hot inner core (home to our vital organs such as the brain, heart, lungs, liver and kidneys), surrounded by a protective cooler shell (our muscles, skin and fat). The hot core is normally around 36.8°C. Even in very extreme climates, that core temperature shouldn't vary by more than two degrees in either direction. If it does, you're in trouble. If your core temperature goes higher than 42.7°C or lower than 28.8°C, you die – either of hyperthermia or hypothermia.

Even at lesser temperatures, extremes of hot and cold can be severely debilitating. It's easier than you might think to succumb to frostbite and hypothermia when you're outdoors in the cold, or to become dehydrated when you're too hot. Later in the book we will deal with how to cope with these problems if you encounter them. But it's much better to avoid them in the first place, which is why it's essential that you have a good working knowledge of how to shelter yourself from the elements. And by shelter, I don't just mean tents and sleeping bags; I mean clothes and footwear too. They are, after all, your first line of defence against the extremes.

It doesn't matter where you are, you need to be
well prepared so the elements don't get the better of you.

FOOTWEAR, ITS SELECTION AND CARE

'A soldier', so the old saying goes, 'is no better than his feet.' It's true. Just ask any member of the armed forces who has served in southern Afghanistan. There, most of the fighting happens in the Green Zone, the lush, fertile area around the riverbanks. The ground can often be marshy and treacherous and, no matter how good the troops' footwear, their skin can remain wet for hours – even days – on end. When it does eventually dry, it becomes cracked and sore. Infection can creep in. Once that happens, you're in for an uncomfortable, painful time.

With a bit of luck, you won't be tramping through the Green Zone. But you will certainly encounter a wide variety of terrains and it's crucial that your footwear should be up to the job. Long hikes can be punishing on the feet. *You* need to make sure that *you* take care of them.

Deal with uncomfortable boots before it's too late. In the military, sunburn is considered self-induced through negligence and is classified as a court martial offence. Likewise, the state of your feet is your own responsibility. So whenever you have a few minutes, dry them, check them and guard them with your life, because as sure as eggs are eggs, life without them becomes much, much harder.

Boots

Regular trainers might seem comfortable (and look cool), but for most outdoor activities they're just no good. They'll absorb the wet, get cold, chafe and collapse. The only time I ever choose trainers for an expedition is if I'm doing a lot of climbing in temperate conditions and I need the flexibility of good cross-trainers. But, as I said, the price you pay is that they get wet easily and tend to stay wet.

A pair of good quality, sturdy hiking boots will last you a long time and keep your feet in good working order. In an ideal world, you'd carry different boots for different terrains, but that's just not practical or affordable. Better to choose an all-round boot.

It's a good idea to choose boots that are about half a size too big. This allows you to wear a couple of pairs of thick socks (important for comfort and to prevent blisters); it also allows for the foot's tendency to expand when it gets hot. High boots that support the ankle are essential in uneven terrain. They need to be strong, but lightweight – a few extra ounces over the course of a full day's hiking can mean you'll use up a lot more energy. Hooks and D-rings are very useful if you're trying to adjust your laces with cold hands.

Leather is the traditional material for boots. It's naturally water-resistant up to a point (much more so if treated) but also allows the perspiration from your feet to evaporate. Some leather boots are lined with material such as Gore-tex, which makes them more waterproof but prevents your feet from breathing. After a long day in the field, this can be a real problem.

It's a good idea to wear your boots in before you spend a serious amount of time with them on out in the field. To do this, put your boots on along with whatever socks you're most likely to be wearing with them, lace them up and stand in a bowl of water for a minute or two. Then walk around in them until they dry. This moulds the boots to your feet as well as loosening the leather and making them more comfortable to wear.

I will never forget my first day of simulated basic training with the French Foreign Legion in North Africa. We were issued with our kit and, before even seeing where we would be sleeping, were ordered out on our first drill – a long route march. We started marching in these hard, shiny, new leather boots, with one pair of very thin socks, across mile after mile of rocky, sandy desert. It wasn't

A good pair of all-purpose hiking boots can mean the difference between success and failure on the trail.

many miles until all of our feet were bloodied, and I have an enduring memory of being part of this hobbling rabble of tough ex-convicts and mercenaries tiptoeing like old women across the desert in agony. It took some of the recruits many weeks to be able to walk pain-free again. I learnt a lesson that day: wear your boots in and never trust the Legion to do it for you.

Socks

Wool is by far the best material for your socks. It will absorb the sweat from your feet and, unlike other materials, it will allow the moisture to evaporate. Always have a spare pair of dry socks in your pack. Never wear socks with holes in them. This isn't just because your mum will tell you off; more importantly, if the material around the hole becomes wet from sweat, it will roll and form a hard ring. The result will be a painful blister. (I once saw a soldier wring blood out of his socks due to blisters. They are not fun.)

Taking care of your feet and footwear

The British Royal Marines, along with most of the world's other special forces including 21 SAS with whom I served, are well trained in travelling long distances by foot. As a result, they have developed a number of techniques for the care of their boots and feet.

- If your boots are wet when you take them off, stuff them with newspaper. Dry them somewhere warm and airy, but not *too* warm or over direct heat as this will dry out the natural oils in the leather, causing it to crack.

- Rubbing wax, grease or dubbin over the laces will stop them freezing should they get wet.

- If your socks (or indeed your boots) are too tight, they will restrict both the flow of blood and the layer of warm air that is between them and your skin. This can lead to frozen feet. And trust me, you *don't* want frozen feet (see page 222 for the lowdown on frostbite).

- Always carry spare socks. If your feet get wet – and at some stage they're bound to – change socks as quickly as you can. If possible, dry out your boots before you put them on again. If you can't then just wring out your socks and wait until the end of the day to replace them with fresh dry ones. (Breathable waterproof socks can also be good to carry as a backup if you are in cold, wet terrain.)

- Wearing two layers of socks is a great way to prevent sweaty feet rubbing against your boots during long-distance hikes.

GENERAL CLOTHING FOR DIFFERENT ENVIRONMENTS AND CONDITIONS

More than anything else, your clothing protects you from the elements. In extreme conditions, the right clothing can be the difference between life and death. Even in more temperate climates, the clothes you wear can spell success or failure for your expedition.

The kind of clothes you need to wear outdoors obviously depends on what sort of weather conditions you are expecting. But no matter what you wear, you need to take care of it. That's why military units, including the US Air Force, teach their soldiers the **COLDER** principle. It's just as useful for civilians as it is for them:

C **Keep clothing CLEAN.** In the summer, this is important for hygiene and comfort. In the winter, clean clothes will keep you warmer. If they are covered in dirt and grease, they lose some of their insulating qualities.

O **Avoid OVERHEATING.** When you get too hot, you sweat – it's your body's natural mechanism for cooling down. The trouble with sweating too much in the field is that the sweat gets absorbed by your clothing, which decreases its insulating qualities. Also, as the sweat evaporates, it cools your body down. Both these facts mean that overheating now can lead to being too cold later, so it's better to avoid overheating by wearing clothes that you can easily loosen or unzip to stop you sweating.

L **Wear your clothes LOOSE and in LAYERS.** The best form of insulation is air pockets. If you wear several loose T-shirts, you will create several insulating layers of what the pros call 'dead air'. These will keep you warmer than one thick jumper, which has no dead-air layers. If you wear a number of layers, it also means you can easily remove something if you start to overheat. And keep the layers loose, because tight clothes restrict the circulation of blood, which will make you cold and numb.

D **Keep your clothes DRY.** Wet clothes can sap your body's warmth, so when you make camp at night, one of your priorities should be drying out any clothes that have become wet, either from the outside (because of rain, snow or frost) or from the inside (because of sweat). Out in the field, it is often difficult to avoid getting wet. Choose a water-repellent outer layer if this is at all likely to happen.

E **EXAMINE your clothes for problems.** Your clothing is going to get some pretty heavy use, so it's important you should keep a keen eye on what sort of state it's in and, if necessary…

R **REPAIR your clothes.** Clothing should be properly maintained and holes fixed as soon as they appear. It's amazing how quickly small holes can become big ones. Once that happens, your clothes will stop doing the job for which you've chosen them, and you lose a key advantage against the elements.

Once you have understood the **COLDER** principle, you can start thinking about exactly what kind of clothes you need to wear for your trip.

*Never forget that your clothes are your first line
of defence against the elements.*

Underwear

Let's start at the very beginning: you need to choose your underwear carefully. Too much, or the wrong type, and you'll overheat and get chafing. Not enough and you'll freeze.

If you are expecting very cold weather, think about thermal underwear that covers your legs and arms. Make sure it's not too tight – this can constrict your circulation and stop it doing its crucial job of delivering oxygen around your body and transporting waste products away from your cells. Stay away from cotton underwear, which is fine in dry conditions but loses its insulating qualities when wet (either from external moisture or sweat). Wool or synthetic materials, from which moisture evaporates more easily, are better.

Don't wear thermal underwear for the sake of it though: if you're out in hot weather, it can be very uncomfortable.

Shirts

Again, you should avoid cotton if you can. Wool shirts stay warm even when wet (it's one of their key advantages over non-natural fibres), but there is also a good range of synthetic fleeces available that are fast drying, warm and in some cases even water- and windproof. One of my favourite items that I often use with a fleece or shirt is a very thin, lightweight windproof top that fits over a fleece and under a jacket. It traps and insulates heat very well, keeps the wind out, but is easy to put on and take off. It also scrunches up into a tiny ball making it light and easy to carry.

Trousers

When you're in the field, your trousers are going to take a battering. They need to be strong, but lightweight and quick drying. Standard issue British Army trousers are good, not least because they have up to ten pockets, which can be useful for carrying things around securely. You should also carry a pair of waterproof trousers. These fit over your ordinary trousers and should be fairly loose so that they don't cause your legs to sweat and also so that you can get them over your boots easily.

Jackets

Think of your jacket as your shell. It needs to be windproof and waterproof; but there are a few other things you should take into account. The jacket should be big enough to allow you to wear several layers underneath in cold weather, and to allow the air to circulate in warm weather. A covered zip will stop the wind and rain getting in. It should also have a waterproof hood big enough to cover a hat; both the hood and the wrists should have Velcro or elasticated cuffs to keep water and wind out and maintain a layer of insulating air within. Make sure you have a pocket on the outside big enough to hold a map.

It might be tempting to buy a jacket in camouflage colours. But what if you get into trouble and people are out looking for you? A brightly coloured jacket means you're more visible to any potential search parties. In a life-and-death situation, it could be the key to survival.

PROTECTING YOUR EXTREMITIES

Gloves

You don't need me to tell you how miserable it is when your hands are freezing cold. Along with your feet, these are the hardest parts of your body to keep warm. We've already talked about the importance of good socks (see page 14). In cold weather, good gloves are just as important.

Mittens are best for heat retention, but have the disadvantage of being a bit fiddly if you need to use your fingers – which you will. It's not a bad idea to wear a pair of thin gloves under your mittens so that you can take the outer layer off and still keep your hands warm. But, watch out, it's very easy to lose or drop your gloves, so you should tie each pair together on a cord that threads through your sleeves. This might sound like something your mum made you do when you were little but I still do this today when climbing. If it's cold and you drop a glove from up a rock face, it can spell the end of the expedition.

I also always take a spare set of inner gloves with me in my pack – just in case. I've had to lend these to people on many occasions when they have found themselves in trouble.

Hats

Hats serve two purposes: to keep you warm in cold weather and to protect you from the sun.

You can lose an amazing amount of heat from your head in cold weather – up to 50 per cent of your body heat at an external temperature of 4°C. The best kind of hat to prevent this is a woollen balaclava that can cover the whole head

A brightly coloured jacket means you can be seen much more easily. Survival matters more than fashion!

in really extreme cold but can also be rolled up to resemble a normal woolly hat. It's not waterproof, but of course you've remembered to bring a jacket with a waterproof hood (see pages 18–19).

Also remember: sun beating down on an unprotected head can cause all sorts of problems such as dehydration, sunstroke and heat exhaustion. A wide-brimmed hat will protect you from most of these. Don't try to be a hero – wear a hat in the heat.

Snoods

A snood, or buff, is a tube of fabric that can be used as head protection against the wind and the heat; a scarf; a wind-protecting face mask; a helmet lining; and even an improvised double mitten. All in all, it is a very adaptable and lightweight piece of gear to have along.

Gaiters

These might sound a bit old-fashioned, but they can be a real help. Made from canvas waterproof materials such as Cordura, they bridge the gap between your boot and your trousers. They are attached to your walking boots to protect your lower leg from thorns and branches, and to stop water, mud or snow entering your boots from the top. They can actually make a critical difference when worn in snow, long wet grass and marshy, boggy terrain. These too go on the 'Bear's vital list'.

THE GOOD PACK GUIDE

There are lots of different packs available, from small knapsacks to big military-style bergens. The size you choose depends on what you're using it for – a one-day outing obviously requires less stuff than a ten-day hike. If you choose a pack that's too big, you'll probably end up filling it with unnecessary items and breaking the cardinal rule of good packing: only take what you really need.

Types of pack

When choosing your pack, there are several things to look out for. The stitching should be good and strong – the last thing you want out in the field is a hole in your pack. Side pockets are useful for items that you'll be accessing throughout the day. A padded waist strap will divert some of the weight from your back to your hips and some packs have extendable lids so that you can increase their capacity if necessary.

The traditional way of mounting a backpack is on an 'H-frame'. But nowadays there are a lot of modern pack frames that are shaped to match the contours of the body. That sounds like a good idea, but people come in all sorts of shapes and sizes. If you go for one of these frames, make sure you try lots of them and choose one that really does fit your own body shape. Remember that most of these packs are designed to fit a male build; women should choose packs specifically designed for females.

Make sure your pack fits well and is comfortable – you might be wearing it through some unforgiving terrain.

The longer you spend on the trail, the more you'll realize what you really need and what you don't.

| How to fill your pack

The most important thing to remember is that your pack should be as light as possible. If you do a lot of walking and you get fitter, you can start adding extra weight to your pack. But remember: just because you carry it easily at the start of the day doesn't mean it'll feel quite so light after a couple of hours' hiking. With the exception of your basic first aid kit (see page 201), you should eliminate anything from your pack that you don't really need. Over time, you'll learn what you need and what you don't, but a basic list should include:

- Sleeping bag
- Tent
- Cooking and eating utensils
- Dry clothes
- Waterproof jacket
- Camera
- Basic first aid kit
- Tinder and fire-making tools
- Food
- Water bottle
- Sharps – knives, axes and saws

You'll probably find that's as much as you want to carry, so leave your iPod at home and listen to the sound of the birds instead.

TRAINING EXERCISES

Good packing is an important skill that can be learned – in fact, new army recruits are taught how to do it in basic training. You should practise doing this at home. Chances are that for each expedition you're going to be packing slightly different things. Make sure you know how it all fits together in the pack so that when you're out in the field it doesn't take long before you are – as they say in the British Army – squared and ready to go. When you think you are ready, test yourself. Memorize where everything is then, with a buddy, try asking each other to find individual items in your pack against the clock... and then do it in the dark.

The Royal Marines issue special guidelines for packing. These are good tips whether you're out on special ops or not...

- Your pack should weigh no more than a quarter of your body weight. Don't fill it with anything unnecessary.

- Keep the pack as high up your back as possible. This keeps your centre of gravity correct and stops the pack interfering with the movement of your legs.

- Arrange items inside the pack so that they are well balanced. Anything hard and irregular, such as tins or shoes, should be kept away from your back.

- Put the items you are least likely to need at the bottom of the pack.

- Wrap everything in plastic bags – no pack is totally waterproof.

- Put items that you are likely to need often in the side pockets. This will stop you having to remove things from the pack unnecessarily.

- Don't be tempted to take your pack off during short stops. Instead, use it as a back-rest when lying down or prop it up on top of a rock or log behind you when sitting down.

TARPS, TENTS, CANVAS AND SHELTERS

Your clothing might be your first line of defence against the elements, but when you stop for the night, you'll need something a bit more robust.

Tents

Tents come in a wide variety of sizes and shapes. Which one you choose is up to you but they're not cheap, so spend a bit of time on research. It's a good idea to match your tent to your environment. A-frame tents are good for moderate, temperate environments and give you plenty of room inside. Mountain tents, walled tents and Lavvus (traditional Sami wigwams) are great for low-altitude, cold environments because you can use a wood-burning stove inside. If you're just going to buy one, a hooped mountain tent is a good general all-rounder.

Most modern tents are very lightweight, so, unless weight is a particular issue, try and choose one that has plenty of space inside. Hoop tents, made from highly flexible telescopic hoops, are more lightweight than frame tents, and

A hooped mountain tent is a good all-rounder and one I've used on many different mountains, including Everest.

easier to erect. Having said that, on Everest I once had to use a self-erecting tent in an emergency. It had a manufacturer's guarantee that it could be erected in under a minute. At 26,000ft, in the oxygen-starved air and in -45°C, it took two of us about 45 minutes. I was never sure whether it was the tent, the altitude or our own incompetence. But the lesson remains: 'Keep It Simple, Stupid'. KISS is a good motto to live by.

Generally tents will have a flysheet and an inner sheet. These serve a number of purposes. The air cavity between the two insulates the tent, making it cooler in summer and warmer in winter. The flysheet protects the inner tent from rain; it also protects it from bird droppings and tree sap. It is possible to buy single-sheet tents, but again you should only consider these if weight is a real issue.

And, of course, always make sure you know how to set up your tent before you go out in the field. You don't want to be scratching your head trying to work it out in the middle of a thunderstorm (or at 26,000ft on Everest!).

| Tarps

A tarp – or tarpaulin – is a sheet of waterproof material that can be used to create a quick and effective shelter, either for spending the night, or simply for protecting yourself from the elements. It has a number of advantages over a more traditional tent.

- It's lighter, so will keep the weight of your pack down.
- If you try to erect a tent in the rain, you're more than likely to get the inside wet. A tarp shelter can be erected much more quickly and, as there is no floor to get wet, rain isn't really a problem. It's quick to dry, too.
- With the addition of lightweight poles, stakes and nylon cordage, tarps can be set up in various different configurations (see opposite), making them potentially more versatile than a tent.
- Cooking under a tarp in wet weather is straightforward and safe.
- Many people prefer the openness of a tarp shelter – you're not enclosed in canvas so have more of a sense of being in the outdoors.

Tarps can be erected in a number of ways. Common configurations include an A-type roof (elevated or at ground level), a lean-to, over a camp cot or hammock, or any combination of these.

I have used tarps in some very obscure, difficult places, from jungles to swamps, and they have been very useful when needing cover in a hurry.

They also provide good space to work in while keeping out of the rain. They don't keep the mozzies out, but a well-placed fire can do that job for you.

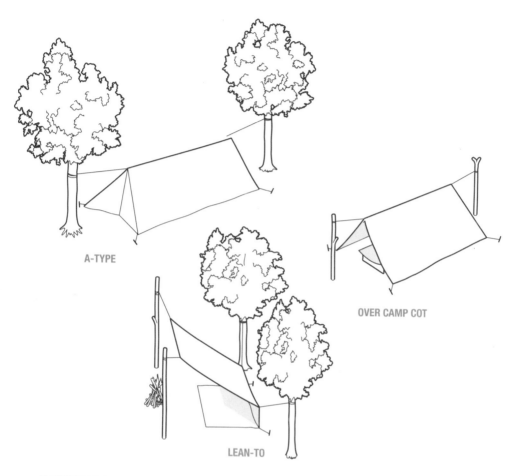

A-TYPE

OVER CAMP COT

LEAN-TO

HIDDEN DANGERS

If you're in an environment where wildlife is a consideration, use a tent rather than a tarp as it puts a wall between you and any unwanted visitors. It may not seem to be a particularly strong wall, but no lions or tigers, for example, have ever been known to rip through a tent purely to get at the occupant. Bears *have* been known to do this, but only when the occupant has made the mistake of taking food into the tent with them – a big no-no if you're in bear territory.

TRAINING EXERCISES

In the military, soldiers practise erecting their tarps and tents as quickly as possible, and so should you. It's a skill you could well be glad of if you need quick shelter when the weather suddenly changes or if you're losing light quickly at the end of the day. The ultimate test is again against the clock and in the dark.

SLEEPING BAGS, MATS AND BIVIS

Sleep is the best natural medicine. Without it, your body will constantly be playing catch-up with itself. When you're out in the field for an extended period of time, it's crucial that you do everything you can to get a good night's sleep. In order to do that you need to be warm, dry and comfortable.

| Sleeping bags

The first decision you have to make when choosing a sleeping bag is whether to go for a down-filled bag or one made from synthetic fibres. Both have their pros and cons.

Down-filled bags are lightweight and have a very good warmth-to-weight ratio. However, they do lose some of their insulating qualities if they become wet – and that includes from the inside due to perspiration. Synthetic materials are more common. They perform better when wet and are relatively easy to dry out. But they are bulkier, heavier and not as long lasting as the down-filled bags. If you're expecting it to be cold and dry (i.e. either in high-altitude mountains or Antarctica) down is the best option; if it's going to be temperate or wet, go for the synthetic option.

Sleeping bags come in different thicknesses to protect you from different external temperatures. There isn't a standardized way of presenting these temperature ratings, but the most common method is a season rating.

1 season bags are suitable for temperatures that do not fall below 5°C

2 season bags are suitable for temperatures that do not fall below 0°C

3 season bags are suitable for temperatures that do not fall below -5°C

4 season bags are suitable for temperatures that do not fall below -10°C

5 season bags will protect you from temperatures as low as -30°C,
depending on the individual bag

It's important to remember that wind and damp air can have an effect on how cold you feel, so if you are expecting either of these conditions, you would be well advised to take a bag with a higher rating than you might normally choose. For most outdoor situations, a 3–4 season rating bag is the best. If you have one with a full-length zip, you can always undo it if you get too hot.

Sleeping bags come in two different shapes: mummy-shaped (thinner at the foot end than at the head end) and rectangular. Mummy-shaped bags are more thermally efficient than rectangular ones because they follow the shape of your body.

One point to remember is that you are always better off stripping down to your thermals before getting into your bag than jumping in with loads of layers

Not all sleeping bags are equal. Try to choose the right one for any given environment.

on hoping to get warm. This applies even if it is really cold. Sleeping bags work more efficiently when there are more air pockets in which to trap the warmth and absorb any moisture you create. If you fall asleep wearing too many layers you overheat, then you sweat, the sweat can't escape, which makes you damp, then you get cold. Then when you wake up cold, you have no more clothes to put on... it's bad all round. So sleep with fewer clothes on and let the air trapped in your bag keep you warm and dry. If you are still cold in the night you can add one layer at a time as needed. I have learnt this lesson through much trial and error.

Mats

You can have the best sleeping bag in the world, but without a mat to sleep on, you're going to be cold. Sleeping bags keep you warm because of the layer of insulating air between you and the bag. The part of your body that is in contact with the ground, however, won't have that layer of air and the cold ground will literally sap warmth from your body.

Any mat is better than no mat at all. Foam mats are warm but uncomfortable. Inflatable mattresses are comfortable but easily damaged. Thermarest mats – a self-inflating mixture of foam and air – are the best. They're more expensive, but will give you that all-important warm night's sleep.

In the Special Forces, where we had to carry minimal personal kit, we used to cut down a foam mat to the shape of our upper torso. This could then be folded up small, tucked in the side of a pack and taken out easily to lie on, either for sleeping or for sitting on during the long hours of an ambush. This would mean that at least our vital organs (in the area around the chest and stomach) were kept off the ground and warm.

Bivis

A bivouac sack – or bivi – is a cross between a sleeping bag and a tent. It's a thin waterproof

A bivi will keep you warm and dry, even in the toughest of places!

shell that slips over your sleeping bag. It increases the ambient temperature by about 5°C and provides protection from wind and rain. It is often used in conjunction with a tarp as an alternative to the tent/sleeping bag combo. This is always my favoured option if travelling light or as an emergency piece of kit: it is adaptable, lightweight and a lifesaver as it can get you out of the wind and rain fast.

LIGHTWEIGHT REPAIR KITS

Like most equipment, repair kits are very personal things. Yours may only consist of a needle, thread and spare buttons. But if you're going to be away from civilization for a while, it's important that you should be able to repair every item you have with you. A more comprehensive repair kit might include:

- Strong sewing thread

- Assorted needles (large, small, curved and straight)

- Spare buttons appropriate to your clothing

- A needle threader – essential for tired eyes, low light and cold sausage-fingers!

- Sticks of hot-melt glue – tubes of glue can burst easily and once you open them the air turns them hard. Hot-melt glue remains solid until heated; when you've finished using it, it reverts to its solid state.

- Sleeping mat repair patches

- Amalgamating tape – rubbery tape with an adhesive backing that amalgamates with itself when you roll it round something, creating a barrier of solid rubber

- Duct tape

- A small sharpening stone or pocket sharpening steel

- A small roll of dental floss – not to please your dentist, but because it makes an excellent multi-purpose thread for heavy-duty repairs

- A container or roll in which to store all of the above

Whether out hill walking for a day or on an expedition to the summit of Everest, having the right clothing and equipment can literally mean the difference between life and death.

There is an old saying, 'you can't talk with experience unless you have experienced'. But this should not always be the case. When Mother Nature is unleashing all her fury and you haven't got the appropriate protection, that experience could end up being your one and only. You should always plan for the environment you are going into, expect the unexpected and take the appropriate clothing and equipment for your mission.

During the first Gulf war, British Special Forces were tasked to go into the deserts of Iraq. Their mission was to send back intelligence on Saddam Hussein's Scud missile launchers that were raining death and destruction down on Israel. A dangerous mission in itself, hundreds of miles behind enemy lines and surrounded by Saddam's own elite Republican Guard. The last thing they expected was to be battling the weather as well. But, as any good Scout knows, you always hope for the best but plan for the worst.

Within hours of being dropped behind enemy lines and commencing their covert infiltration on foot, the soldiers were caught out by unexpected bad weather, including sub-zero temperatures and even snow – in the desert! Snow was not on the mission briefing, but they had planned well and were carrying the right clothing and equipment to combat the severe weather. However, in the pitch black of the night, one soldier became disorientated and was separated from his patrol.

When hypothermia sets in, it does so quickly and can take you unawares. One minute you are shivering, the next you have lost the use of your hands through cold and your mind stops functioning clearly. Sadly for this soldier he became a victim of the freak bad weather and died. But the other soldiers survived by having the right kit and, just as importantly, knowing how to use it before things got out of control.

It may be bright and sunny when you plan your hike into the mountains or your next camping expedition; but Mother Nature can change her plans very quickly. Don't let this spoil your trip. As the famous Scout saying goes, 'be prepared'. Then you stand a fighting chance.

TOOLS
OF THE TRADE
using and maintaining your lifesaving sharps

If you are out in the field for a long time, you're going to struggle without a good blade, or even several of them. They are essential for so many jobs: chopping firewood, cutting your way through thick undergrowth, clearing a space to make camp and even for fashioning other tools. A lot of people get by with just a Swiss Army penknife. That's better than nothing, but it isn't a real alternative to good, sharp knives, axes and saws. Whether you are able to take all three of these on every expedition obviously depends on how much other gear you plan to carry. But you should know how to choose, use and look after your lifesaving sharps. A tool is only as good as the user – so practise. And don't forget the golden rule of sharps: the tool should be doing the hard work, not you.

KNIVES

Of all the cutting tools you take with you, none will be as helpful as your knife. You can use it to make fire, to construct improvised shelters and to find food. In short, it's one of the most important objects you can carry with you. But in the wrong hands, sharp knives can be extremely dangerous. If you're going to carry one, you need to be well versed in all aspects of knifecraft.

Knives come in all shapes and sizes.
Remember: they're tools, not toys.

Choosing your knife

A good general-purpose knife will have a blade that is about as long as the width of your palm. Many people, however, prefer to carry two knives – a smaller one and a larger one – so that they can have different tools for different jobs. Good knives don't come cheap, but if you can afford two, you'll probably find them to be more useful.

The first decision you have to make is what kind of blade you want. Generally speaking, there are two choices: stainless steel or carbon steel. Stainless steel knives are less expensive and will not rust, but they are difficult to sharpen and will not keep their edge for very long. Carbon steel blades sharpen easily and good quality ones will keep their edge for longer. However, they will tarnish and possibly rust, so you will need to clean your knife regularly and take good care of it even when, after a period of years, it develops its own protective patina – a dark film of oxides and carbonates many metals acquire over time. If your knife gets rusty, clean it with an emery cloth or other abrasive, then lightly oil it to keep the rust from returning.

When blades are made, they undergo a heating and cooling process known as tempering. Tempering a metal makes it harder or softer according to the speed at which it is cooled. The softer it becomes, the less brittle it will be. Make it too soft, however, and the blade will not keep its sharpness and may snap if you use it to lever something open. The hardness of a blade is measured in Rockwells. A good all-purpose knife will be somewhere between 55 and 62 Rockwells. If you decide to take two knives with you, it's a good idea for the larger one to be harder than the smaller one so that you can use it to lever things open without breaking it.

The curve of the blade's cutting edge should extend the whole length of the blade. A curved blade will cut well and is the best shape for effective sharpening. The point of the knife should be sharp enough to stick into wood without too much effort. Some knives have a guard between the blade and the handle to stop the hand from slipping on to the cutting edge. But this is not really necessary, as that only happens when you make a stabbing movement, which you shouldn't if you're using your knife correctly.

The blade and handle of the knife should be made of one solid piece of metal to stop it weakening at the join. The handle, however, should have a good comfortable grip attached to it, preferably moulded so that it fits your hand. Wooden grips can be cut away to make the shape more suited to your own hand.

HIDDEN DANGERS

Knives with folding blades can be very handy, but be careful. It's easy to close the blade accidentally on your fingers, which will have you turning straight to the first aid chapter (see pages 198–225), or going immediately to the hospital if you've chopped your fingers off! If you do have a folding blade, don't be tempted to use it to lever things open. This will weaken the hinge and make the knife less safe.

Sharpening your knife

It's essential that your knife is extremely sharp, both for practical and safety reasons. A blunt knife that slips when you try to cut with it is a hindrance and a hazard, not a help. A sharp knife, on the other hand, needs less pressure and so keeps you in control. Remember that a knife that is too blunt to cut paper cleanly is too blunt to cut through wood.

When a knife is blunt, it means the cutting edge has become rounded. Your aim is to make the edge sharp and chisel-shaped. To do this properly, you need to follow a five-stage sharpening process: on a coarse sharpening stone, a medium sharpening stone, a fine sharpening stone, a hone and a strop. If you were to look at the knife under a microscope after using the coarse sharpening stone you would see that it had rough teeth, like a saw. It might feel sharp to the touch, but as soon as you use it these teeth are going to fold over and it will become blunt. The further you go through the sharpening process, the smaller these teeth become. Your aim is to have the blade look like a microscopic razor, not a microscopic saw. Sharpening a blunt knife for the first time is a long process; once you've done it, however, it is easy to keep it sharp with good maintenance.

Stages 1–3

Your sharpening stones should be moistened before use to stop the microscopic bits of metal that you are filing off your blade from clogging it up. Stones that you keep at home can be lubricated with oil, but out in the field it's best to use water. Once a stone has been used with oil you can't use water on it; however, if you have used water on a stone it can be thoroughly dried and converted to an oil stone.

Start with your lubricated coarse stone. Set the knife at about a 10° angle with the blade facing away from you. In one smooth movement, drag the edge

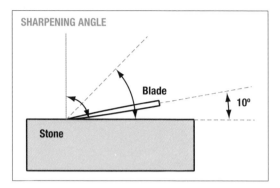

SHARPENING ANGLE

Blade

10°

Stone

away from you along the stone, ensuring that you grind the entire length of the blade. Now turn the blade over so that the edge is facing you and repeat the stroke coming towards you. Make sure you keep the same angle at all times.

Once the edge feels sharp, you can move on to the medium stone. Repeat the process, and then move on to the fine stone. You'll learn by experience when the time has come to move from one stage to the next, but five minutes on each is normally sufficient.

Stages 1–3 of the knife-sharpening process should be performed at home or at base camp as the sharpening stones can be heavy and cumbersome. Honing and stropping can be done in the field. You can also avoid having to perform stages 1–3 too often by honing and stropping on a regular basis. It's a good idea to have your honing rod and a belt that can be used as an improvised strop on you or in your pack at all times.

SHARPENING
STONE MOVEMENT

Stages 4–5

Once the knife edge has been ground on a fine stone, you need to hone it. A smooth ceramic sharpening rod is best for this. Again, you should make sure that the angle is kept constant and that you sharpen the whole length of the blade, with the sharp edge leading.

The process of honing will provide a very fine edge. However, the edge will be *so* fine that it will produce what is known as a burr. A burr happens when the thin, flexible edge bends over. If you were to leave the burr and cut with the knife now, it would tear off, taking part of the blade with it and blunting your knife again. This is why stage 5 – the strop – is so important.

A strop is usually made of a leather strap – a belt works well. You remove the burr by dragging

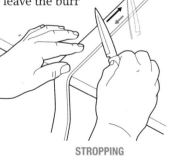

STROPPING

IMPROVISING IN THE FIELD

If you don't have a sharpening rod with you, try to find a smooth boulder in a riverbed and use that to hone your knife. I have often had to use this technique in the field and with practice it works well.

each side of the knife along the strop (keep the blade as flat as possible to avoid damaging the material). You tend to need a lot of strokes on the strop, but it will ensure that you have a very sharp blade that, most importantly, stays sharp.

Making camp in a swamp is always hard, but without a decent knife it is always an awful lot harder.

TRAINING EXERCISES

Sharpening stones are expensive and you can damage them if you don't grind your knives at the right angle. However, you can practise your knife-sharpening skills by sticking different grades of abrasive wet/dry (waterproof) sandpaper on a board. Once you've mastered the techniques, you can move on to proper sharpening stones, which should last a long time if used properly.

Safe use and stowage

Fixed-blade knives should have a sturdy leather sheath so that they can be safely stowed in your pack or on your belt. Your knife should be sheathed whenever it is not in use. Make sure you always know where your knife is – it should be on your person or in your pack. The last thing you want is for it to fall into the hands of someone who doesn't know how to use it safely (or actively wants to use it irresponsibly), or for it to get lost. Remember that you are the guardian of a dangerous weapon and you need to treat and guard it with the same level of respect and responsibility a soldier does with his rifle. Real men don't act all butch with their weapons; rather they carry them discreetly and use them wisely.

When removing the knife from its sheath, hold the sheath by the flat edge. Never curl your fingers round the whole sheath: it is quite possible for the sharp edge to cut through the leather and then through your skin.

If you need to pass the knife to somebody else, hold it with the blade pointing upwards and towards you. Above all, however, you should never walk with an unsheathed knife. It's very easy to trip out in the field; if that happens when you're carrying an unsheathed knife, it becomes a lethal weapon, dangerous both to others and to yourself.

When you are using a knife to cut anything, you must always be aware of where the knife is going to go if it slips. You should never rest anything over your knees to cut: the insides of your thighs are full of arteries. Just one cut in the thigh area and you could bleed to death. It is much better to rest whatever you are cutting against the side of your outstretched leg and cut away from

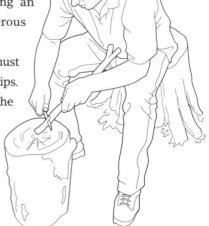

HIDDEN DANGERS

If you're stropping a folding blade repeatedly, be especially careful that you don't accidentally activate the hinge and close the blade on your fingers. I did this once when I was a kid. Ow! Lesson learnt.

your body. If you are performing a cutting task that needs to be done in front of you then sit down, put your elbows on your knees and again cut away from your body. An improvised chopping block in the form of an old tree trunk is useful for resting your piece of wood; if your knife does slip, the block forms a safe barrier.

Whenever you're using your knife, make sure you *concentrate*. If anything is distracting you, stop cutting and wait for the distraction to pass before you continue. Never use a knife when you're tired. And finally, don't use your knife when the light is bad. When the sun goes down, it's time for your knife to go to bed too.

AXES

A good axe is a very useful tool in the field, especially when it comes to chopping firewood. It can also be used for campcraft projects: removing branches from felled trees and carving heavier objects such as ash tent pegs. Like knives, however, axes can be very dangerous in the wrong hands. If you're going to take an axe with you, you need to know how to wield it.

Choosing your axe

Axes come in a pretty bewildering range of shapes and sizes. As a general rule, the bigger the axe the safer and easier it is to use, though, of course, they can be unwieldy and heavy. So when you're choosing an axe to take with you on an expedition, there's going to be some element of compromise. Some people recommend choosing an axe in the following way: hold the head in your hand with the handle going along the inside of your outstretched arm; it should just reach your armpit. It's not a bad technique, but don't worry if you think an axe of that size is too big to carry with you. You'll probably find that the most you want to carry is a small hatchet, or hand axe, weighing between 500g and 1kg. You won't be able to use this to cut down big trees, but it will chop smaller branches more easily than a knife, and once you get used to

handling it you'll be surprised at how versatile it can be. Just remember that you're more likely to do yourself an injury with a smaller axe because the blade is closer to your body.

When choosing your axe, have a good look at the blade. Axe blades come in three different shapes – convex, concave and straight. Each blade is good for different tasks. There are a number of axe styles and everyone has their own preferences. For me, the best all-round axe would be a half axe, also known as a small forest axe, with a slightly concave blade with a slightly rounded edge.

Convex blades

A convex blade is good for splitting logs. If it's too convex, however, it won't cut very deep, meaning you have to put more energy into the swing. This is something you want to avoid. After all, the tools should be doing the hard work, not you.

Concave blades

A concave blade is useful for stripping branches from trees or larger logs. It should give a good deep cut. If it's too concave, however, it will be difficult to pull out of the wood. Again, this results in you expending too much energy.

Straight blades

A straight blade is less likely to slip from the surface of the wood you are trying to chop, but it's more of a specialist tool used for big projects like cabin building.

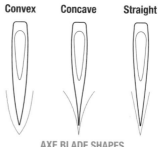

Convex   Concave   Straight

AXE BLADE SHAPES

The shape of the cutting edge – whether it is rounded or flat – is important. Think of a rounded edge as being like the point of a knife: it will cut deeper than a flat edge, which is designed to give a neater cut. For general purposes in the field, a rounded edge is likely to be of most use.

Sharpening your axe

A blunt axe is little more than a hammer. It has to be sharp if it's going to be any use at all. The principles of sharpening an axe are the same as those for sharpening a knife, but the technique is different. With a knife you move the blade over the sharpening equipment; with an axe you move the sharpening equipment over the blade. This means that the blade stays still and your hands move. For this reason you should always wear a sturdy pair of gloves when sharpening an axe. Also, don't be tempted to place the axe on your knees – remember those arteries between your thighs? At home, place it on a table; in the field you should kneel down with the axe raised on a tree trunk or other object in front of you.

You can buy special tool sets for axe sharpening. These consist of an axe file, a diamond file and a stone with a rough and a smooth side. Each of these elements is used for the four stages of sharpening an axe.

Stage 1

You only need to perform this stage, known as 'cutting back', if the edge of your axe is severely damaged. The process of cutting back removes quite a lot of metal from the blade, so you don't want to do it too often. You're going to be pushing your axe file towards the cutting edge of the blade, so *make sure you're wearing sturdy gloves*.

With the blade in front of you, turn your file at a 45° angle and raise the far end slightly. Move your strokes along the blade as you file so that you cover the whole length of the cutting edge; then turn the blade over and repeat on the other side. Keep going until any nicks are ground away, remembering to work each side equally.

Stage 2

Take your diamond file and set it at an angle opposite to that used in stage 1. Repeat the filing process until you have removed any marks left by the cutting-back process. Again, stage 2 may be omitted depending on how blunt your blade is.

Stage 3

Stages 3 and 4 are where your axe is going to become really sharp. You should do this regularly to keep it in top condition.

Take the rough side of your sharpening stone and moisten it with some water. Holding it at an angle to the blade, start sharpening in smooth, circular movements in a clockwise direction working from left to right. You will find that a rough paste starts to accumulate on the blade. Don't wipe this away: this abrasive paste will help sharpen the axe. Turn the blade over and do the same on the other side, then repeat until you have a good sharp edge.

Stage 4

You're now ready to hone your blade. Use the smooth side of your sharpening stone, again in a circular motion. This time, however, sharpen in an anticlockwise direction moving from right to left.

▏Safe use and stowage

Before you start chopping wood, you need to mark out a safe area in which to do it. Make sure that you are well away from other people – especially younger children who might be overly inquisitive about what you're doing. Make sure there are no overhanging branches, and whatever you do, don't try to use your axe in an enclosed space. You need room to work: if you're cramped, you're dangerous.

In order to use your axe safely, you need to make sure you are using the right tool for the right job. A small hatchet of the size you are likely to be taking with you is suitable for trimming small bits of firewood, thin branches and twigs. Don't try to use it to chop anything much more than about 8cm in diameter: for larger pieces of wood, the correct tool to use is a saw (see pages 48–9).

Before you start, make sure you are not wearing any loose clothing, like scarves or lanyards, which can get in the way. Always make sure you're wearing sturdy boots – an axe will make short work of soft shoes. Ensure that there are no tree branches or anything overhanging that might get in the way of your strokes. Check the axe before you use it. If the handle is at all damaged or the head is loose, don't risk it. You should also check that the axe head and handle line up. If they don't you may find that your axe strokes are dangerously out of control.

A small hatchet should be used one-handed. Use your other hand to hold the piece of wood you are chopping. Never ask someone else to do this because you need to know that the wood is secure at the moment the axe hits. Rest the wood you are chopping on some sort of block – again, a tree stump is good – and make sure the part of the wood you are cutting is over the block. You don't want the axe to slice through the wood into thin air or into the ground. If your cutting block is low down, kneel in front of it to make yourself more comfortable.

Make a dummy stroke first, just to double check there's nothing in the way. Think carefully about what will happen if you miss the wood. What will the axe hit? A finger? Give yourself plenty of room for error. Fingers don't grow back, so use your common sense.

Don't try to bring the axe down at right angles to the wood as this could make it bounce back up. Instead, make your first cut at a 45° angle. Your second cut should be at the same angle but from the opposite side so that you chip out a V-shape in the wood. Continue this process, making the V-shape wider and wider until the wood has been cut in two.

TRAINING EXERCISES

There is a skill in using an axe to strike a piece of wood just where you want to. A good way of practising at home is to mark a piece of wood with some chalk. Try to get your strokes as close to the chalk mark as possible.

Using an axe can be exhausting. If you're feeling tired, stop. If you don't, you're much more likely to make a mistake.

To carry an axe safely, hold it by the head with the blade facing forward and the handle up towards your armpit. That way, if you fall, the blade will go safely into the ground. Camp etiquette states that you shouldn't really borrow someone else's axe; but if you do want to pass your axe to someone, have them stand to one side of you, facing in the same direction. Give them the head of the axe first.

As with your knife, don't even think about trying to chop wood if you don't have enough light. Never leave an axe lying on the ground: it could easily slice open someone's foot if they were to step on it. The best place to store your axe is in a spare tent reserved for tools, if you have one, where it will be safely out of the way and protected from the weather. Failing that, you should drive your axe into the top of the stump of a dead tree so that the blade is out of the way. Don't be tempted to drive it into a living tree: you will damage the tree and the axe could easily become dislodged and fall on someone. In the absence of a tree stump, you should lean it up against a tree trunk with the head on the ground. It's possible to buy a leather sheath for your axe, but even if you have one of these you need to be careful as it can split if your axe is as sharp as it should be.

When stowing your axe away between expeditions, keep it out of the elements, but not somewhere so warm and dry that the handle shrinks in the axe head. Make sure that the axe head is not wet when you put on the sheath; it's a good idea to grease the head with oil so that it doesn't go rusty.

BEAR'S SECRET SCOUTING TIPS

Don't discard the chippings that come away as you are chopping wood. They make very good kindling for the fire.

SAWS

An axe and a saw work well together, but an axe is more adaptable. When limited to just one tool many people will choose an axe. But if you can take a saw with you as well, you'll find the work involved in cutting up firewood is much reduced. They are also very handy for precision cutting when you're making camp furniture. And saws are much safer than axes and are useful to have around for emergencies. When you're tired, cold or the light is failing and you absolutely have to cut wood, a saw is your best option.

Choosing your saw

There are two types of saw that you are most likely to encounter: a collapsible saw and a bow saw. The collapsible saw is like a folding knife. It is very lightweight and can fold away safely and conveniently in your pack. It's small, discreet and good models can be locked in both the open and closed positions. It is, however, less sturdy than a bow saw. This has a bigger, stronger blade connected at both ends by a hoop of metal – rather like a large hacksaw without the handle. If you're going to take a bow saw, you need to choose one that will keep the blade under a high level of tension. Bow saws can be bulky and heavy to carry; but bear in mind that the energy you expend on carrying a saw will be more than recouped when you start using it.

Sharpening your saw

Unlike a knife or an axe, saw blades can be easily replaced – this is true for both folding and bow saws. It is possible to sharpen a very blunt saw back to its original keenness, but this is a very detailed, seven-stage process. If your saw has become completely blunt, it's probably best to replace the blade.

Safe use and stowage

A sharp saw, used properly, should stay in good condition for a long time. If your saw is of good quality, the blade and the teeth should be totally straight. The key to using your saw effectively is to avoid forcing, twisting or bending the saw in any way. Make sure you're comfortable and have plenty of room around you. Let the saw do the work. The strokes you use should be fairly gentle, allowing the sharpness of the teeth to cut the wood rather than your own exertions.

The wood you are cutting should be held firmly in place. If you need to use your hand for this, keep it as far away from the blade as possible. Start your strokes slowly until you get up a rhythm. Try to use the full length of the blade: short strokes are less effective and you'll end up using more energy to do the same work.

When your saw is not in use, the blade should always be covered, either with a clip-on mask or with a length of material tied round the blade. And as with all sharps, never leave a saw lying around.

Real-life campfire story

Having the wrong tool for the job can be as bad as having no tool at all. Knives, axes and saws come in all shapes and sizes, and it is very important that the tool or tools you choose to take on your expedition are the right ones for where you are going and for what you intend to use them. And remember, all tools have their limitations. It's no good trying to fell an oak tree with a penknife.

During one phase of UK Special Forces selection, the recruits spend many weeks in the jungles of Borneo, an extremely demanding environment that will challenge the hardiest of souls and the hardiest of tools. Here, as well as their personal weapons, the soldiers are equipped with a parang – a jungle machete – as well as a small folding saw. In the hands of an experienced person a parang is a most versatile tool, capable of felling large trees or making intricate, precise cuts when building traps or constructing a camp. But it is also one of the most dangerous bushcraft and survival tools if used incorrectly, as one young medic who was attached to the SAS discovered on the selection course.

While building his A-frame bed, he decided he was going to need some small poles to help stretch his tarp out taut to allow the rain (of which there is an abundance in the jungle) to run off. Armed with his parang he confidently strutted off into the forest in search of his poles.

Had he been a seasoned jungle soldier he would have known that firstly, a blunt parang is a lot more dangerous than a sharp one and secondly, a machete, although the tool of choice for many jobs, was not necessarily the right tool for this one. Once he had identified his poles he set about trying to chop them down but soon found that in the close confines of the jungle it is not always possible to swing a machete fully due to the dense undergrowth. Getting very frustrated that he was unable to chop even the smallest of sticks, he started to slash at them harder and harder. Now, had his parang been sharp and in the hands of someone who was familiar with its use, it would have cut through the small branches like a hot knife through butter. Unfortunately it was blunt… very blunt.

He did eventually manage to make a cut: through the small cluttering sticks, through his chosen pole – and through his camouflage trousers, with the blade finally coming to a halt firmly embedded in his knee. Why? Because it was blunt, and because he consequently had to use excessive and uncontrolled force. As he was unable to use his parang effectively in the close confines, he should have opted to use his saw. Instead he ended up being evacuated to the nearest hospital by helicopter.

Knives, axes and saws are not inherently dangerous; it is the user that makes them so. They need maintenance, they need cleaning and they need sharpening, but above all they need practice in their safe use. Do this and they will serve you well and make your time in the outdoors more comfortable, enjoyable and easier going.

And finally, don't be a knife nerd. A knife, axe or saw is there to serve you. It is not a status symbol or trophy to parade around. They are just tools to help you perform tasks in the wild, simple as that. Look after them, learn how to use them, always respect them and they will serve you well.

Chapter 3

CAMPCRAFT AND PIONEERING

making yourself secure in the field

There are few things that feel as good as the sun on your face, clean mountain air in your lungs and sleeping under a bright, star-filled sky. But the sun does not always shine and rain clouds often obscure the stars. Nature, in short, is not always your friend and you need to make sure you are properly sheltered and secure in the field. Any fool, as we used to get told in the military, can be uncomfortable.

In this chapter we will discuss not only how to choose the best campsites but also the different kinds of shelter available to you, both man-made and natural. Then I'll give you some tips on how to construct shelters by using some of the abundant materials the natural world has to offer.

CAMPSITE SELECTION

When you're out in the field, chances are that you'll spend more time in your tent than in any other single place. You'll sleep in it, use it as shelter from bad weather, rest in it and – depending on what type of tent it is – cook your meals in it. So it makes sense to ensure that you pitch camp somewhere suitable. A few minutes checking the ground and the surroundings could save you a lot of aggro later on. Few campsites are a hundred per cent perfect (that's half the fun of the wild), so you'll always have to compromise a bit, but these are the main things you need to think about when selecting your position.

| Slope

It goes without saying that you'll get a better night's sleep on flatter ground than on a steep slope, but that's not the end of the story. A very gentle incline will allow rainwater to drain away from the campsite and stop it from becoming a boggy nightmare. If you do find yourself camping on level ground, try to choose an area where the soil is capable of absorbing any rainwater. A good way of judging this is by driving a tent peg into the ground: it should be soft enough to take the peg, but not so marshy or wet as to swallow it. If you camp in a dip, you might find the area prone to mist and midges. Higher up is better, but not so high up that your tent poles attract lightning in a storm. (I once met a man in the Costa Rican jungle who had been struck by lightning while in his tent. He told me how he covered his face in terror, but the flash was so intense he had actually seen the bones of his hands through his closed eyes. He was very lucky to have survived.)

Air and wind

Before you pitch camp, try and work out which way the prevailing winds come from. You want the back of the camp to face the wind so that the camp itself provides shelter. Try not to camp somewhere too exposed, as severe winds can be devastating to a camp (and storms always seem to happen at 3 a.m. when you are cosy in your sleeping bag!); but equally, try to make sure that there is enough space around your camp to allow the sun to dry the ground after a rainstorm and for air to circulate freely.

| Supplies

Nothing is going to wear you out quite so fast as having to walk a long way carrying wood or water. If you can, camp near a decent supply of both.

| Safety

Although it's a good idea to be near a wood supply, you don't want to camp near dead trees, or even live trees that have big, overhanging, old-looking branches. In a storm, these can easily break off and fall. The same is true of trees that are leaning precariously in your direction.

If you're camping on a slope, check uphill for any loose boulders. And make sure you're far enough from any stream or water source that might be in danger of flooding as a result of heavy rainfall.

Most animals will avoid you, but it's worth a quick check that you're not camping too close to any animal runs or holes.

PITCHING TENTS

Once you have decided on the general location of your camp, it's worth taking a little bit of time to lay it out properly. Make sure there's enough space between tents for privacy (people are always secretly grateful for their own personal space); and work out where specific features such as the camp kitchen or the woodcutting area are going to be.

Lay out your groundsheet, but don't start hammering your pegs in yet. First of all, examine the area under the groundsheet very carefully. Remove any stones, twigs or knobbly bits and do it thoroughly: they might look just like little pebbles now, but after several hours of lying on them you'll feel like you're sleeping on Stonehenge! (I have often been guilty of overlooking this task when tired at the end of a long day, and I always regret it.)

Once the ground is cleared, stake down the corners of your tent before erecting the poles or hoops. You can then readjust the corner pegs to make sure everything is in its proper place, before inserting the rest of the pegs and covering with the flysheet. You should be able to tell just by looking at it whether your tent has been properly erected: the shape will be symmetrical and the canvas taught and wrinkle-free. The flysheet and the inner sheet should not be touching; if they do they lose their waterproof properties.

It's a bad idea to set up camp so close to a white-water river – flash floods can occur quickly and without warning.

NATURAL SHELTERS

Tents – especially modern ones – are brilliant. But you don't always have one. Maybe you've been stuck out in the wilderness. Or maybe you really want to go old school and back to nature and construct your own shelter from the materials at hand. This is always the most fun and rewarding option. It adds an exciting dimension to your trip, and it's a great skill to learn.

The easiest kind of natural shelter is the one that's already there. Unfortunately, suitable natural shelters can be few and far between, and even

If you're smart, use what nature provides as shelter from the elements.

if you are lucky enough to stumble across one, you need to be aware of the difficulties they can present.

Caves

Caves might seem like the ideal natural shelter. After all, they've been there for thousands of years and the earliest humans used them as dwelling places. And it's true that a good, dry cave can be a great place to stay. But most caves are not like this. They're often wet and cold and once the sun goes down they can be impenetrably dark. Sounds a bit less enticing now, doesn't it? If you light a fire in an unvented cave, it will become full of lingering smoke. You also need to be careful of caves that play host to crowds of bats. There is a fungus present in their droppings that can cause a sometimes-fatal illness called Darling's disease – a decent reason to avoid bat pooh (or bird pooh for that matter). And, of course, in some parts of the world, there are vampire bats, which will suck your blood during the night without you even feeling it. They inject an anti-coagulant that means you stream blood, and they target the soft areas like your eyes, head and fingers. A friend of mine woke up with his hair soaked in blood after being bitten by vampire bats. This can be an annoying way to start the day!

Overhanging cliffs

Again, these aren't very common but they can provide good shelter, especially if they are south facing – i.e. into the sun. If you decide to set up camp under a cliff, you can estimate how much protection you'll get during a rainstorm by feeling the ground. If it's damp, chances are you will be too! Because of their situation, cliff overhangs can be draughty. (This is called the Venturi effect, which is where wind speeds up as it gets compressed when it hits a cliff face.) If you have the materials available, you can protect yourself from the winds by building low walls around you; if not, a warm sleeping bag or bivi could save you from a cold night's sleep.

Tree canopies

If the canopy overhead is thick enough, it can be sufficient to protect you from all but the fiercest rainstorms, but it can only really be a short-term shelter. Don't write this option off, however: it can be a lifesaver and can relieve you of hours of unnecessary work if you get the right trees. Remember: the smart Scout uses what nature has already provided.

MAN-MADE SHELTERS

From the simplest wigwam to the tallest skyscraper, all man-made buildings essentially do the same thing: keep the rain out and the warmth in. You don't need to be an architect to create simple shelters, and if you can master a few basic principles, you'll be amazed how versatile such man-made shelters can be. All the shelters described here are designed so that the rain runs off their roofs. Dig a ditch about a hand's span depth around your shelter and you will avoid being flooded from the outside.

But here's a word of advice before you start. The following shelters all have one thing in common: they need basic materials, mainly logs and foliage, which you're most likely to find in a forest. Even if you have to go some distance out of your way to find woodland to shelter in, it's worth it. You'll more than make up for lost time by having the materials close at hand.

Lean-tos

There are two basic lean-tos: the fallen-down-tree lean-to and the open-fronted lean-to, both well suited to any environment where there are trees.

The fallen-down-tree lean-to

The fallen-down-tree lean-to is probably the simplest man-made shelter you can create. It also has the advantage of not needing any ropes or cordage.

Stage 1

As the name suggests, the first thing you need to find is... a fallen-down tree! In woodland areas these are very common, but try and find one that's the right size (of course, a suitably shaped boulder can perform the same job). The tree forms the high wall of your triangular lean-to. If it's too low you won't have much space and water will drain away less successfully; if it's too high you might have difficulty insulating the open ends. Aim for a height of about a metre.

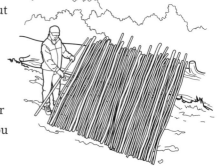

Stage 2

The roof of the lean-to is constructed using long, straight branches – either windfalls or, if necessary, ones that you have cut from existing trees. These should be laid close together so that there are as few air gaps as possible.

Stage 3

Once you have constructed the basic shape, you need to insulate the roof. There are all sorts of materials you can use to do this: large bits of bark, leaf mould from the forest floor, even branches thick with leaves. Don't cut corners when you're doing this: these materials are going to keep the rain out and the warmth in. Cover your lean-to well, and try to arrange the materials much as you would tiles on a roof, with the upper ones overlapping the lower ones (i.e. start from the bottom and work upwards). This will help the rain run off the roof without leaking into the shelter.

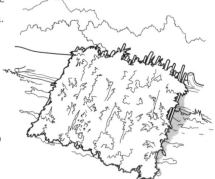

Stage 4

Once the roof is finished, you need to block off one of the open ends to prevent drafts. If you're expecting the weather to be particularly cold, you can block both ends of the lean-to to increase its insulating properties. Use the same materials as you did for covering the roof, or alternatively build a 'wall' of logs.

The open-fronted lean-to

Open-fronted lean-tos are very well suited to cold, dry environments because they rely on a fire built on the open side for their warmth. The heat radiates inwards and reflects down from the roof. The downside, of course, is that they are less suitable for wet weather, or when you're staying somewhere you can't light a fire.

The principle is the same as the fallen-down-tree lean-to but, in the absence of a fallen tree, you need to construct something sturdy enough for the slanted roof to lean against.

Stage 1

To make the frame, you need to locate a straight branch that is taller than you, two straight poles about 3 metres long, and two upright poles about 1.5 metres long, preferably each with a forked end. Construct the frame as shown, tying the joins tightly with rope or whatever cordage you have at your disposal (see pages 64–70).

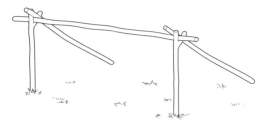

Stage 2

Collect enough long, straight branches to create the lean-to roof as shown below. You want the roof to be at an angle of between 45° and 60° (don't worry; you don't need to get your protractor out – remember the rule of thumb, 'near enough is good enough'!).

Stage 3

Now cover the roof with the same insulating materials you would use for a fallen-down-tree lean-to (see page 61). Remember, the more thorough you are at this stage, the warmer and drier you'll be. Cover each end of the lean-to with insulating material as well. If your roofing material is lightweight, you can weigh it down with some more branches in case the wind picks up.

Stage 4

A fire is crucial to the success of an open-fronted lean-to. As you'll be lying down, you want to make sure that your fire is the same length as you are if you're going to stay properly warm. (See Chapter 4 for the lowdown on firecraft.) If you're building more than one open-fronted lean-to, position them so you have two facing each other – that way two people can share the heat from one fire. Both of you can help keep the fire stoked during the night, and, of course, it is more sociable.

Tripod shelters

Tripod shelters – or wigwams – are one of the oldest kinds of man-made shelter. The large style of shelter that you might be familiar with from stories about Native Americans are good, sturdy structures; but because of their size they can be difficult to cover and thatch, which makes them less well suited as short-term shelters or in inclement weather locations. However, a three-pole shelter can be a useful alternative to the other lean-tos described here: it doesn't require a fallen-down tree and, if properly constructed, it can offer more insulation than an open-fronted lean-to.

Stage 1

Locate a long, straight branch that is slightly taller than you, plus two shorter straight branches. The size of these smaller branches will depend on your own size: the finished shelter needs to be just big enough for you to fit inside when lying down. Construct the frame as shown, tying the joins tightly with rope or whatever cordage you have at your disposal. It is best to tie all three poles together at the top when the poles are laid down; then splay them out afterwards. This will ensure the knot remains good and tight.

Stage 2

Collect enough straight branches to line the walls of the shelter as shown below. Remember to place these as close together as possible to increase insulation and stop water leaking in.

Stage 3

Cover the tripod shelter with leaves, foliage or whatever natural insulating materials you can find. Make the covering as thick as possible.

CORDAGE, KNOTS AND LASHINGS

Tying knots is one of the most useful skills you can learn for when you're out in the wild. But before you tie them, you need something to tie and there's a limit to the amount of rope you can reasonably carry with you. If you're going to live successfully in the wild, therefore, you need to be able to make your own cordage – another word for thread, string or rope. Happily, it's a lot easier than it sounds; and it can be more versatile than you think. Natural cordage can be used for shelters and other campcraft projects; it can also make bow-strings, fishing lines, snares and even 'cotton' for sewing. All in all, it's a skill worth learning.

Almost any fibrous material can be turned into decent cord. If these cords are long enough, they can then be plaited into quite sturdy ropes. But first you need to gather your supplies. In your search for suitable cordage material you need to consider four things:

1. Is the material *long* enough? The process of turning a fibre into rope will shorten it so it needs to be quite long to start with.

2. Is it *strong* enough? Once the fibre is twisted and plaited it will strengthen, but it should be reasonably robust to start with. To test its strength, give it a sharp tug. Then twist it and rub the fibre between two fingers. If it doesn't break, tie a simple knot and tug it tight. If the fibre still doesn't break, it should be strong enough.

3. Is it *flexible* enough to work with? You're going to be doing a lot of twisting!

4. Will the fibres *grip* on to one another? If the fibres are too 'shiny', they won't.

This might sound like quite a demanding list, but, in fact, natural materials that match these requirements are reasonably common: tall grasses; weeds such as stinging nettles (grip the nettle at the base of the stem, pinch your fingers together and run them up the length of the stalk – the leaves will all come off without stinging you); seaweed; fibrous materials from the stalks of certain shrubs; even the moulted hair of animals. Probably your best source of cordage material, however, comes from the inside of dead tree bark, particularly willow and lime. Simply loosen the fibrous material at one end of the bark and pull it off in long strips. Then separate these strips until you have lengths of the required thickness.

You should also bear in mind that most natural fibres will shrink as they dry, which makes the weave looser. However, some materials can be more difficult to process once they are dried out. A good compromise is to soak dry materials in water before you process them: they will shrink a lot less than when they dry from their natural state. (This process is called 'retting'. If you take pieces of bark off young lime, willow or sweet chestnut trees and soak them in a river for a while, the natural fibres will free themselves from the bark. If these are left to dry they will be soft, pliable and ready for use.)

Once you have your raw material, you need to process it into something useful. There are lots of different ways of doing this. The method I'm going to explain to you is very easy, and will produce versatile cordage that you can use in all sorts of situations.

Making your own laid cordage

Laid cordage is the term for any rope made from fibres that are twisted together.

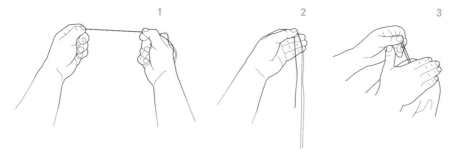

Stage 1

Take a long, single fibre. Twist it repeatedly in one direction until it naturally wants to form a kink.

Stage 2

Fold the fibre about a third of the way along. Don't be tempted to fold it in half, as this will give you a weaker finished product.

Stage 3

Grasp the fold between the finger and thumb of one hand. Place the doubled-over fibre on your lap and use the palm of your free hand to roll it one full roll away from you. You are not trying to make the fibres overlap at this stage; just aiming to twist each strand individually.

Stage 4

Keeping your palm firmly held down, to stop the cord from untwisting, release your other hand. The cord should twist neatly.

Stage 5

Pinch the cord where the twisting ends and repeat the process until you are 4–5cm from the shortest end. To continue, lay another strand of fibre up to the shortest end and 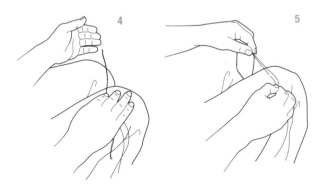 carry on the process as before – the new fibre will automatically entwine itself into the existing cord. When you've finished rolling the cord, just tie it at the loose end to stop it unravelling. If the cord is too thick to do this, you can tie a separate piece of cord round the end instead.

Your finished cord will be substantially stronger than your original fibres, but you can make it stronger still by folding over the existing cord and repeating the process. If you do this, make sure you roll the cord in the opposite direction to the way you started.

So, you've made your cordage. Now you need to know how to use it. Generally speaking, a cord is no use unless you've got a few knots up your sleeve. There are literally hundreds of different types of knot, and you could spend half a lifetime learning them all. You're better off learning a few, and learning them really well, then getting out and using them! If you learn the knots listed below, you should always find you know one that performs the job you want to do. Here they are, then – Bear's Top Ten knots.

TRAINING EXERCISES

You can practise this process easily at home without having to go out and forage for materials. Just use lengths of thin string (you can cut out stage 1 of the process). You'll be amazed how quickly it turns something insubstantial into something very sturdy.

Bowline

This is probably the most useful knot you'll ever learn. It's used to form a loop at the end of a rope. It can be tied very quickly and it won't slip or tighten. There's a useful mnemonic you can use to remember how to tie it.

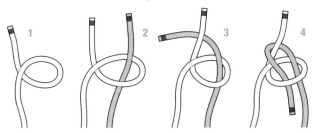

1) The rabbit hole 2) The rabbit comes out 3) It runs round the tree 4) It goes back down its hole

If your life depends on a bowline, add a half hitch in the working end when finished. This makes it a hundred per cent secure.

Buntline coil

Not so much a knot as a convenient way of storing your rope without it getting all tangled up.

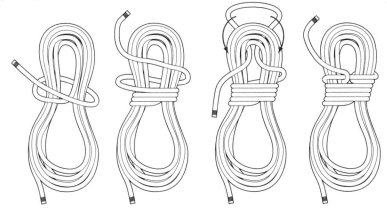

Clove hitch

Use this to attach a rope to a horizontal pole or post.

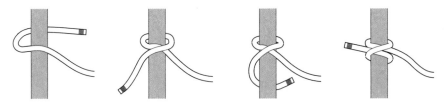

Constrictor knot

This is really useful for tying the neck of a bag or sack.

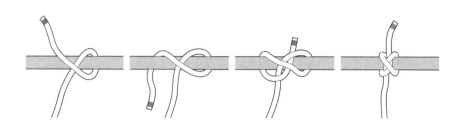

Figure of 8 loop

This knot is easy to learn, reliable and – crucially for a good knot – easy to untie. It is a very popular knot with climbers and sailors, but you can bet you'll find a use for it in the field. It is particularly useful when the final loop can be passed over a post.

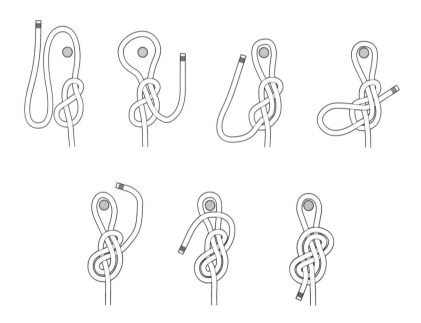

Jam knot

Also known as the locking knot, this is a good knot for general construction, as it can bind two sticks together tightly. This knot is a faster and simpler version of the sledge knot but once you've tightened it, put a couple of half hitches at the end so it can't ever work loose.

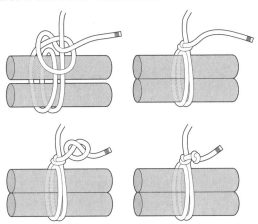

Sledge knot

This is the ultimate construction knot, you can put a radiator hose in a car with it and it will hold. However, you cannot undo this knot; you will have to cut it if you no longer want to use it.

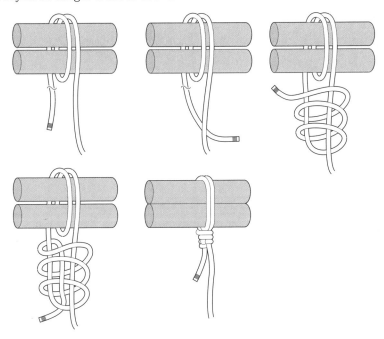

Reef knot

One of the most common knots, and used to tie two pieces of rope together *provided they are of equal thickness*. It's easy to untie. Add a half hitch to each end if you need to make it a hundred per cent secure.

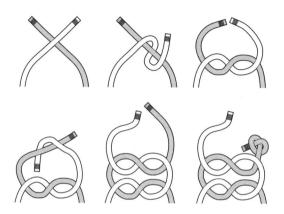

Sheet bend

This knot performs the same function as the reef knot, but this one works for ropes of different thicknesses.

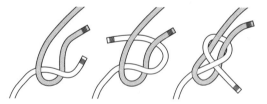

Timber hitch

This is a good temporary knot for dragging wood or other objects, and also as a general lashing. It will tighten when under strain, but comes undone easily when the rope is slack.

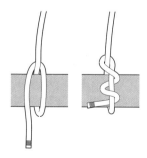

CAMPCRAFT PROJECTS

If you're staying in one camp for a while, it is always worth spending a little bit of extra time adding a few simple creature comforts. I'm not talking about a TV, but more fundamental things like beds and washbasins. Obviously you can't take the kitchen sink with you when you're out in the field; but with a little ingenuity it's amazing what you can create using easy-to-find, natural materials. You'll probably discover that you won't have time to make many of these projects for one-off, overnight stays; but for longer-term fixed camps they can make your life a lot easier and more comfortable. With campcraft projects there are no hard and fast rules: you'll find yourself improvising and adapting all the time and that, of course, is half the fun. But to get you started, here are a few ideas.

A camp bed

Chances are that you'll have some sort of inflatable mattress with you, and, if you've read my tips on page 30, you'll know that it's essential to have something to keep your body off the ground. However, an inflatable mattress can absorb water – not a big issue if it's being used in conjunction with a bivi bag (see page 30–1), but a potential problem if you're just sleeping under a tarp. Even if the air cavity keeps this moisture away from your body, it's annoying to have a wet mattress: when you roll it up for storage it can become mildewed and unpleasant.

The solution is to improvise a camp bed, which is a lot easier than it sounds.

Stage 1

Find a couple of substantial logs about a metre long and place them parallel to each other at your head and foot positions, about 15cm away from the top and from the bottom of your mattress (so, if you have a 2-metre mattress, place them 2.3m apart).

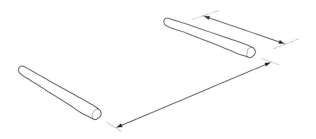

Stage 2

Now find several long, straight branches about wrist thickness and support these on the logs, securely fastened with a timber hitch (see page 70) to form a raised platform. Alternatively, use your knife to cut notches in the end logs on which the poles can rest without moving. You can now lay your air mattress on to your wooden platform and you'll be raised from the ground.

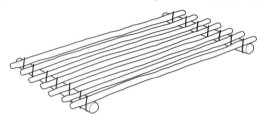

▎A camp table

A camp table can be a real asset, for obvious reasons. A table is little more than a raised platform: as long as it's flat enough, the stump of a tree will do the job. But if you're in camp for a few days, you'll probably find that you want something bigger and more permanent.

If the ground is suitable, you can make a good camp table by digging two trenches opposite each other, then putting the displaced soil along the outer edges of the trenches to use as seat backs. The bit in the middle forms the platform or table.

The following drawings show a really good way of constructing a wooden table with seats. Don't worry if the wood you find isn't as neat and straight as the wood you see in the picture – (it never is!) – but try and get it as straight

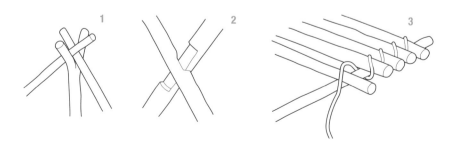

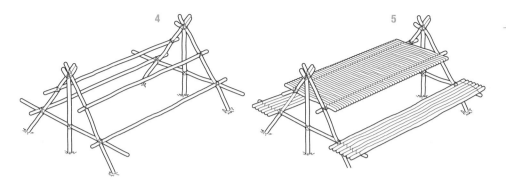

and as balanced as possible. Don't be afraid to use your sharps to cut the poles to the right size and to indent the poles where they join. Use a sledge knot or jam knot (see page 69) to lash the poles together.

Camp chairs

Camp chairs can be invaluable, especially if the ground is soggy. With a bit of practice, you can construct a camp chair in about 15 minutes. Just follow these diagrams. The secret is to find three sturdy forked branches that you can cut into the shapes shown here. Once you have constructed the frame, cut yourself some shorter branches and lash them to it using a sledge knot or jam knot (see page 69).

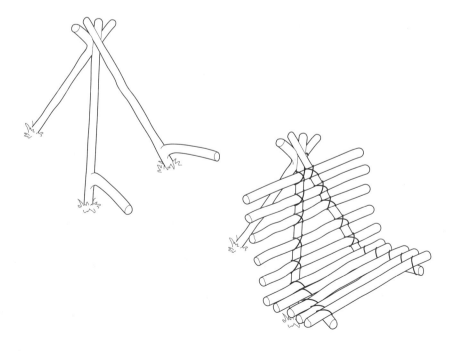

| Camp lights

We're so used to being able to flick a switch to turn on a light that it's easy to forget how dark it can be outside at night. This is especially true in the jungle where it gets pitch black in minutes when the sun goes down, as all natural light is lost in the dense canopy of jungle foliage. I have been caught out on several occasions by not being prepared enough by sundown. Trying to make camp in the jungle, in the dark, is hard work!

I once made camp in the Transylvanian mountains, which have the highest population of bears in Europe. Only a few hours earlier I had encountered, at close quarters, a huge brown bear, which only served to make me even more determined to make sure my camp that night was as safe as I could build it. I rigged up a simple trip-wire perimeter all around my small shelter. If this was triggered it would dislodge my mess tin that was full of stones and suspended up a tree. At one point in the night I was certain that I heard a noise and went out to check the perimeter wire. But it was absolutely pitch black and I had no torch, and in the process of checking the wire I triggered it accidentally. I almost jumped out of my skin when the stones came crashing down around me, piercing the silence of the night. Sometimes our imagination is our own worst enemy!

If you've got a fire going, that will give you a bit of light; and a torch is good for directional light, especially in an emergency. It's a great idea, though, to carry a few candles with you. Candles don't stand up by themselves very easily, however. A good trick is to stick your knife into a tree trunk, flat side up. Melt a few drops of wax on to the blade, then stick your candle on to it. (Alternatively use melted wax to stick your candle on to any flat surface – just make sure it's well away from anything flammable.)

But what if it's windy? I'm going to show you a neat way of using a glass bottle to make a candle-holder that will keep the wind out. To do this, you

BEAR'S SECRET SCOUTING TIPS

Don't throw away butt ends of candles or the wax that drips off them. They can be melted down into an empty tin can with one end cut off. Insert a small piece of string into the melted wax, let it harden and you've just made yourself another camp light (and a potential lifesaver if you run out of other light sources).

need to cut the bottom off an empty glass bottle. Sounds impossible? Bear with me! With care, this can be done safely in the field without any fancy equipment. All you need is a thin piece of wire, a fire and cold water. Heat the wire until it's red hot then, using gloves to protect your fingers, tie the wire around the bottle where you want to cut it. Plunge the bottle into the cold water and it should break cleanly and easily. Push your candle into the ground (or you can use the melted wax technique to stick it to something) and then place the bottle upright, over the candle. Hey presto: a wind-proof lantern!

A washstand

If you're on an expedition with a group and one of you has brought along a lightweight bowl, it's straightforward to construct a stand for it so that you have a raised washbasin. Arrange the three poles in a tripod formation about 30cm from the top using a sledge knot or a jam knot (see page 69). The bottom parts of the poles will form the legs, while the top parts make a cradle for your bowl. (For a more elaborate camp washstand suitable for longer-term fixed camps, see page 127.)

IMPROVISING IN THE FIELD

If you don't have a bowl, a piece of tarpaulin can be laid over the cradle of a tripod stand with a length of cordage wrapped round to secure it. This will make a simple, improvised camp washbasin.

Real-life campfire story

There are many extraordinary stories about feats of endurance and survival in which intrepid explorers like Scott and Amundsen have battled with the elements, or wartime prisoners have escaped across hostile jungles and mountains. These can be spectacular examples of fortitude and determination. But the truth is that you don't have to be on an expedition in the Antarctic to find yourself in a survival situation. It can happen right on your doorstep. Having a small amount of simple, logical knowledge – such as how to tie a few knots or use certain materials to make shelters, fires and rope – can save you a lot of misery.

A friend of mine was on Special Forces selection. Having completed the first few stages, he found himself on the run during what is now called the SERE phase – Survive, Evade, Resist, Extract. This wasn't in some frozen wasteland or in the jungles of Borneo, but in the hills and valleys of North Wales!

Pursued by the hunter force, whose job it was to search for and capture the SAS hopefuls, he found himself charging through a dense coniferous forest with men and dogs hot on his heels. Running through a region of closely planted trees, he didn't have much opportunity to assess his situation or select his best route. He found himself bursting out from the treeline and jumping straight into a pond. He had got away but it was October, and the water was sufficiently cold to knock the air from his lungs.

The mercury had dropped well below freezing on the previous four evenings and the wind was blowing. He soon realized this could rapidly turn into a life or death situation. Lighting a fire wasn't an option, as it would alert the hunter force to his whereabouts. His only alternative was to construct a shelter to protect him from the biting wind and

The thick canopy of the forest meant there was not much undergrowth. He clawed away at the forest floor to assess the depth of the spruce needles – about 45cm – not enough to get him below ground level. He needed to build upwards but had no rope or building materials with which to do this.

As he'd been digging, however, he'd come across a number of spruce roots. The spruce root is one of the best naturally occurring materials for tying knots. When split down, they are ideal for lashing together a temporary lean-to shelter. My friend rapidly started to unearth as many roots as he could. He split them down and then collected dead branches from the forest floor. In next to no time he had constructed a low, tactical shelter. All he had to do now was pile spruce needles and forest debris over the windward side and his shelter was complete. Suddenly, a night in the freezing temperatures, in the dark, when soaking wet and in a gale, was survivable.

Necessity, as the old saying goes, is the mother of invention. In other words, if your need is great enough, and you think long enough and hard enough, you can eventually come up with a solution to a challenge – even if you have to improvise materials and tools. You don't need yards of nylon cord and tarpaulins in the wilderness; with a bit of common sense you can not only survive, you can make yourself very comfortable.

You may not be in a survival situation, but in the field there are always going to be times when you need to improvise. You'll soon realize that the natural world is your outdoor shop, hardware store and tool shed all rolled into one. And all it requires from you is the willingness to get in there, think smart, smile and never give up! That's the scouting way.

Chapter 4

FIRECRAFT

mastering the art of making and maintaining a campfire

Fire is your best friend in the field. It provides heat, it cooks your food, it gives you light and – just as important as all these – it keeps your spirits up. Man has always had a fascination with fire, and of all the skills of the outdoorsman none seems to be more important than the ability to create it. That said, making a good fire is a bit of a mystery to many people. If you and your friends are going to enjoy successful expeditions then this is one craft you must not fail to master.

There are three important things to remember before we start to discuss the art and craft of firemaking:

1. Fires should only ever be lit in designated areas or with the landowner's permission.

2. Small fires are better than big ones. They provide plenty of concentrated heat, but they are easily controlled. A campfire is not the same as a bonfire. Big is not necessarily beautiful.

3. Never forget the three Ps: preparation, preparation and preparation. If you try and rush a fire, it will go out. Simple as that!

THEORY OF FIRE

Why does a wood fire burn? It might sound like a simple question, but if you've ever sat in the cold, labouring over a couple of smouldering logs, I bet it's one you'll have asked yourself (or probably more pertinently: why *doesn't* this thing burn?!). Well, when it comes to firelighting, a little bit of science goes a long way. The people who know most about fires are firemen, and they have constructed a simple model that explains what a fire needs to burn. It's called the fire triangle.

The fire triangle explains that there are three ingredients necessary for a fire: fuel, heat and oxygen. If you take any one of them away, your fire will go out. We'll look at each of them in turn.

Fuel

Without this, there is no fire. In the field, your fuel source is most likely to be wood. Different woods burn at different rates and temperatures.

Heat

It's really important to understand that without an initial level of heat, fire cannot begin. This is because heat transforms solid fuel into gas. It's this gas, mixed with oxygen, that causes a flame.

Oxygen

A fire won't start without oxygen. If the oxygen is then depleted, the fire will reduce to glowing embers. Reintroduce the oxygen (imagine blowing on the coals, or using a pair of bellows) and the fire will reignite. You need to ensure, therefore, that air can circulate in and around your fire.

A knowledge of the fire triangle will directly affect your firelighting skills. I want you to imagine taking a match to a piece of straw. It will burn, right? Now, imagine taking a match to a thick log. It won't burn. This is because the small flame of the match does not provide enough *heat* to raise the temperature of the log sufficiently to turn it to a gaseous state, but it does provide enough for the small piece of straw. Point of the story? When you're lighting a fire, always start with very small pieces of fuel. As they burn and the heat increases, you can slowly add larger pieces. And always make sure that nothing is packed so tightly that the air can't circulate. 'Overworking' or smothering a fire is a common mistake for inexperienced firelighters.

HOW TO LIGHT A FIRE

Now that we know the theory of fire, we can put it into practice.

Preparing your location

There are a few things to consider when choosing where to lay your fire. It's important to be near a source of fuel. If the weather is fine and there's not much wind, you can light your fire almost anywhere; but if you're not so lucky, look for some kind of natural shelter: a clump of trees, a cliff or even just a big rock. Make sure that there are no low overhanging branches, or anything nearby that will ignite should the fire give off any sparks.

When you've decided where to lay your fire, you need to prepare the ground by scraping it clear of anything that will burn, such as leaves or dried grass. If the ground is very wet then build up a base of live wood on which to construct the fire. This can be a series of small green branches, roughly 60cm long, laid next to each other like a grill. Having this base will help the air circulate under the fire and won't burn through easily so will remain in place as your hearth. If it is very windy you can dig a shallow pit in which to make your fire. This will protect it from the wind, and is especially useful when you are starting it. I have used fallen tree trunks to shelter a fire, and have even made small, contained fires *in* the fallen tree trunks themselves. But remember, any fires started against fallen trunks must be carefully monitored and properly extinguished afterwards. Dowse with water from a nearby stream, or pee on it!

Remember: when you're lighting a fire, *you* need to be in control. Random bits of flammable material lying around are a hazard, so make sure to remove them before you start.

Collecting your materials

Tinder

Tinder is fine material that lights easily and provides enough of a flame to ignite smaller pieces of kindling wood. Natural tinders include the tops of dead weeds, birch bark, pine cones, dry bracken or grasses – even dry orange peel or an old empty bird's nest. Anything that you can put a match to and be sure will ignite. (Some people suggest using dry leaves, but I find they tend to smoulder rather than provide flames and heat.)

One of the best natural firestarters is pine resin. This is a kind of sap found under the bark of pine trees. It often seeps out from damaged areas of a pine tree. If there are fallen pine branches lying around, cut into the knotted areas and you'll find sap-soaked wood; or collect small amounts of sap from a number of live trees.

Never use paraffin, petrol or meths to light a camp fire. They're dangerous, and you don't need them.

The shavings from bark make good tinder.

BEAR'S SECRET SCOUTING TIPS

Tinder is light and doesn't take up much space. If I find good tinder when I'm out in the field, whatever time of day it is, I grab it and put it in a dry pocket. This means that if it rains later on I know I have some reliable tinder with me with which to start a fire. If it's already raining then grab some wet tinder anyway and put it in your pocket – it should dry out next to your body as you walk. If it's been wet all day and it's probably going to rain tomorrow, once you have a fire going, take the opportunity while you have a supply of heat to dry out a good batch of tinder to carry with you. That is called smart scouting!

Think how much wood you're likely to need, then treble it!

Kindling

Once you have your tinder, you need to collect some kindling wood. The best place to source this wood is from dead branches that are still on the tree as they tend to be drier than branches on the ground. You want thin bits of wood 30–40cm in length. If you can't find small branches, use your sharps to cut down larger pieces of wood.

Good woods for kindling include birch, cedar, cypress, Douglas fir, holly, larch, silver fir and yew. If you can teach yourself to recognize a few of these, you'll be at an advantage. A Scout trick to recognize good kindling is to snap a twig: if it makes the crackle of a wood fire, it is dry and dead – good for kindling. If it bends or snaps weakly, it is still damp inside or is living, and therefore no use.

IMPROVISING IN THE FIELD

If you can't find any natural tinder, use your knife to shave wood off a larger log and cut it into pieces no bigger than a match. You'll need a good handful of this improvised tinder to start a fire. Good non-natural tinders include: cotton wool (check it isn't the non-flammable type before you go out in the field though!), tissue paper, paper, cardboard and a Vaseline-impregnated piece of card. You can also use the inside of a tampon, although some of them are now non-flammable so you should check before you go.

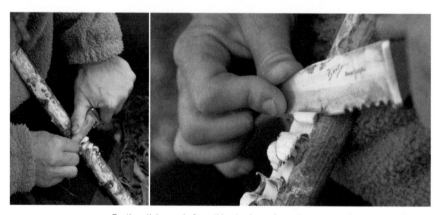

Feathersticks made from thin shavings of wood are an excellent source of tinder.

Larger fuel

Don't be tempted to light your fire until you've collected your larger, slower burning logs. Split these logs into various thicknesses so that you can continue the process of increasing the size of the wood you add. Split logs will burn faster than round ones, and smaller pieces more quickly than larger ones. Think what sort of fire you want – a merry blaze or a slow burner – and prepare your wood accordingly. Most importantly make sure you have enough reserves so that you don't need to go wood gathering at the wrong moment (like at 2 a.m. in the middle of a freezing cold night!). And remember: however much wood you think you will need for the night... treble it. You will be grateful you remembered this tip when the fuel supply has almost completely disappeared by dawn! Once, when I was sleeping in a cave in Siberia during winter (about -35°C at best), I had a fire going and gathered what I thought was enough wood for three nights. By dawn I had burnt through all three nights' supply – easily!

Laying your fire

There are lots of different ways of laying your fire, but they are all designed to ensure that the fire triangle is maintained. I'm going to show you three good methods: the tepee fire, the star fire and the criss-cross fire.

Tepee fire

Place your tinder in a pile and arrange your kindling around it in a tepee formation, making sure there's enough space between the wood for air to circulate. Once the fire is burning, add your heavier wood in the same formation. If you have the butt end of a candle, you can place this in the middle of the tepee under your tinder. It will create a constant flame and make your firelighting more reliable.

Star fire

Take four logs, place them in a star shape as shown which allows only the ends to burn. Push each log further towards the fire as needed. As the heat source in a star fire is very focused, it is very useful as a cooking fire for a small pot. This is a great fire if wood is limited and you need to conserve your fuel source. One drawback is that it does not give out much heat.

BEAR'S SECRET SCOUTING TIPS

There's nothing more useless than a wet match, but out on the trail it's a problem you might encounter. Matches can be dried sufficiently by rubbing them through your hair, but you can also waterproof them before you leave home by dipping them one at a time into melted candle wax. (I used to do this a lot as a young Scout and on more than one occasion I was grateful out in the field!) Alternatively, a cigarette lighter could turn out to be your best friend. In an emergency, don't forget every schoolboy's favourite trick of concentrating the sun's rays through a magnifying glass. The heat produced is easily enough to get fine tinder going. You can perform the same trick with any piece of glass that has convex sides – like some old bottle bottoms.

Criss-cross fire

Take two heavier logs and lay them parallel to each other. Put the tinder in the middle and then lay a criss-cross pattern of kindling as shown. Once the fire is going, you can continue with this pattern, using heavier bits of wood as you go.

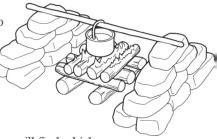

I like the criss-cross fire best. Over time you will find which fire works for you. It is fine to have a preference – Scouting is there to make individuals of us!

Lighting your fire

Once you've laid your fire and made sure you have enough fuel to hand, you can light it. If there is a breeze, crouch down in front of the fire so that your body acts as a windbreak. Strike a match to the bottom of the tinder, not the top.

A firesteel and striker is a good way of getting a fire going – and this method can't break, unlike a lighter!

LEAVE NO TRACE – THE IMPORTANCE OF EXTINGUISHING YOUR FIRE CORRECTLY

A lit fire should never be left unattended. It only takes a gust of wind to blow a spark on to something flammable and you've got a disaster on your hands. You should therefore extinguish your fire whenever you leave camp.

TRAINING EXERCISES

In an ideal world, all fires would be lit using perfectly dry tinder and kindling of exactly the right sort. Unfortunately it doesn't always work out like that. It's worth practising your firelighting skills using different materials, including some that aren't perfectly dry. If you can hone your skills before going out in the field, you'll find life much easier. And being able to light a fire quickly and with whatever materials come to hand can be a lifesaver.

I did once admit defeat when I was in the middle of the Ecuadorian jungle and it had been pouring – I mean *torrentially* pouring – for two days solid. Everything on me was soaking wet and the rain was so strong that you could hardly even hold a conversation. I tried and tried, with good tinder, matches and even a lighter. But there comes a time when you need a change of plan. I spent that night huddled at the bottom of a tree, trying (pretty unsuccessfully!) to keep warm with thick bunches of grasses stuffed down my trousers and shirt.

If you are leaving the camp temporarily, then stamp out the fire. Be very careful to make sure it is completely out. But if you are leaving the camp permanently then your best means of extinguishing a fire is, of course, water. If there's a stream nearby, any large logs that are still smouldering should be thrown into it. If not, use a bucket or whatever receptacle you have to hand to soak it from all sides. You should stamp upon and soak any embers. Then, soak the earth around the fire so that any smouldering embers that remain don't get the chance to spread.

If there's no water available, you need to starve the fire of oxygen (remember the fire triangle?). This can be done by covering it with sand, gravel or loose earth. Pile it high so that the fire is *completely* covered.

Whichever method you use, don't leave camp until you are absolutely sure that the fire is extinguished. It doesn't take much for wildfires to start in forests or dry grasslands – or indeed anywhere that things will burn. You must take special care if you are in an area with a lot of coniferous trees or wherever the ground has a peat substratum. In areas like these fire can spread underground and pop up somewhere else up to a year later.

And finally, you should make a point of keeping the means to extinguish your fire to hand all the time. Even the best-laid fire can be unpredictable if there's a sudden gust of wind, especially in very dry weather. Respect your fire. It's an elemental force and can be very, very powerful. I once had to run through a forest fire in Alabama as part of a programme on surviving a forest blaze. The guy I was leading wore contact lenses and they melted in his eyes! And that fire was a baby. Don't underestimate the power of a wildfire.

It's crucial you extinguish your fire. I've been in the middle of a controlled forest fire, and it's no joke.

Real-life campfire story

Fire can be our friend, but out on operations with the army, it can also be the enemy, as it can alert an adversary to a soldier's presence. However, when the guys come off the ground, the opportunity to have a hot brew and some food is always high on everyone's list – once the kit's been sorted, the weapons have been cleaned and all the admin is complete, of course!

One of my good friends from the SAS was once tasked to a situation with a foreign group of soldiers, and he ended up witnessing the longest fire-making attempt in the history of mankind! A patrol had been out on the ground for several days. They had the bare minimum of rations owing to the amount of operational equipment they had to carry. In such circumstances, luxuries get struck off the list and food often falls into that category.

Back at base camp, they quickly set about making a fire to get some food on the go. In their eagerness to get some hot scoff inside them, they forgot the basics of firelighting: preparation, preparation and preparation. They decided they could outwit physics and go from fine grass tinder to huge logs in one easy step. That was their first mistake! It was a painful business as they tried again and again. They ran out of tinder and even began painstakingly extracting belly button fluff in order to get the fire going once the grass had run out. Eventually my friend could watch no more and intervened to help them out. Sometimes you have to learn from your own mistakes, but a wise man learns from the mistakes of others.

Had these guys understood the principles of fire, they'd have had hot food in no time. As with all survival skills, we should learn, practise and perfect them well before we need them. That is the key to good scouting. Remember the three Ps of firelighting next time you're in camp and are tasked with getting the supper fire going: it will then be quick and effortless and you'll be everyone's new best friend!

CAMP COOKING

the skill of preparing, storing and cooking your vital fuel

They say that an army marches on its stomach, and it's true. Without fuel inside us, we eventually grind to a halt. You and I need food like cars need petrol; and like cars, the further and faster we go, the more fuel we use up. A car with a heavy roof rack will use fuel at a higher rate, just like a person with a heavy backpack. At home, you might be able to manage for hours on a bowl of cornflakes and a cup of tea, but when you're exerting yourself outdoors, that won't last you very long at all.

If you're going to spend any amount of time in the field, it's crucial to understand what kind of food will provide your body with the essential energy it needs. And if you're going to *enjoy* your time in the field, you need to become proficient at camp cooking. Decent food is a great morale booster. Eating the same thing day in day out can really get you down (just ask any soldier who's been forced to survive on army ration packs for a while); whereas a bit of inventiveness at the campfire can make your day a whole lot better.

HOW YOUR BODY USES FOOD

You body converts the food you eat into three main categories – protein, carbohydrates and fat – which are then broken down to provide energy and waste matter. The name given to these two processes is metabolism.

For our purposes, we can think of metabolism as doing two things: it maintains our body heat and it provides the energy our body needs in order to carry out its essential functions. Active muscles metabolize food faster than inactive ones. This is why sportsmen and women need a higher food intake than, say, people who work in an office. Their metabolic rate is higher. And if you're walking for miles with a heavy pack, or living outdoors where the temperature is cooler, your metabolic rate is going to be pretty high too.

The proteins, carbohydrates and fat from which our bodies derive their energy are present in different foods in varying ratios, as are other important constituents such as vitamins and salt. If you have a basic knowledge of what these different food groups do, you'll have a better understanding of what makes up a balanced diet.

Fat

We all know that too much fatty food can be bad for you. But fat provides almost twice as much energy as carbohydrate or protein. Your body also needs it to absorb certain fat-soluble vitamins (notably carotene, A, D, E and K). But – and this is a big but – there are good fats and bad fats. It is important to know and understand the difference.

Saturated fats are, on the whole, the ones to avoid. They raise your total blood cholesterol and can lead to heart disease. Saturated fats are mainly found in animal products such as meat, dairy and eggs. Mono- and poly-unsaturated fats, on the other hand, lower your total cholesterol and can be found in foods like nuts, avocados, salmon and olive oil. Let's take an avocado, for example (an all-time favourite of mine!). They get a pretty bad press

because everyone thinks they're fattening. But the fat in an avocado is entirely good for you. Such fats, in fact, as well as lowering our total cholesterol, are essential for our immune function, lubricate the joints and provide us with the basics for healthy hair, nails and skin. So know your fats and remember that good fats will keep you healthy while bad fats will make you fat! A good rule of thumb is that the fats that go solid and white at room temperature are bad and the fats that stay runny are good. If you're inactive, fat shouldn't constitute more than a sixth of your food intake; but if you're exerting yourself, it can constitute up to a third.

Carbohydrates

These fall into two groups – simple and complex. Simple carbohydrates are also known as sugars. They will provide energy, but it won't last. Deriving your energy from sugar is a bit like trying to heat your house by burning newspaper: you need a lot of it, because it burns so quickly. It's much better to use a fuel that releases its heat slowly. That's where complex carbohydrates come in.

Complex carbohydrates are found in food such as wholemeal bread, brown pasta and rice, wholegrain cereals, root vegetables, pulses, nuts and, best of all, oats. They are easy to digest and provide a speedy, longer-lasting source of energy.

The right combo of healthy food will keep you going further, for longer.

About half your daily intake of food should consist of complex carbohydrates. I use oats in almost everything: they are shown to be cancer-preventing, cholesterol-lowering and are packed with essential minerals and vitamins, as well as providing long-lasting, slow-release energy that avoids the peaks and troughs of simple carbs and sugars (such as white pasta and white bread).

Protein

The body needs protein for healthy cells and muscles. Protein also provides energy in about the same quantities as carbohydrates. Traditional protein-rich foods include meat, chicken, fish, eggs and milk; but health-wise you are better off getting your proteins from natural wholefood sources such as pulses, nuts and even good old oats again! In general, in the West, we are led to believe we need much more protein than we actually do. In fact, you are better off eating more fruit and vegetables and good wholegrain carbs. Do this properly, with a generous sprinkling of nuts and pulses added to your stews, and you will be getting more than enough protein already.

Vitamins

These are compounds that are required in tiny quantities for metabolism and general good health. The fat-soluble vitamins mentioned on page 93 can be stored by the body and so don't need to be eaten every day. The eight

BEAR'S SECRET SCOUTING TIPS

If you're worried about vitamin deficiency, remember that green grass contains vitamins A, B and C – and it doesn't actually taste all that bad!

B vitamins and vitamin C, however, are water-soluble; as such they should be consumed daily from a natural wholefood source such as green veggies and good fruits.

Salt

Too much salt is very bad for you; too little, and you can die. Salt is an electrolyte – a mineral that can dissolve in water and carry electrical charges. Pure water doesn't conduct electricity; salty water does. Your body needs tiny charges of electricity for all sorts of purposes, including carrying messages along your nerves and controlling your heartbeat. All in all, salt is pretty important.

When you're out in the field, you sweat. Your sweat contains a high concentration of this essential salt and, particularly in hot climates, salt deficiency is something you need to look out for. It's easy to spot – cramps, dizziness and nausea are all symptoms – and easy to remedy. If it is very hot and you are sweating a great deal, drinking a lot of water and eating non-salty, natural foods, you might want to add a sprinkling of salt to your main meal, or have a few salted nuts as a snack, or use the occasional rehydration sachet. But on the whole, remember you will generally be getting plenty of salt from the foods you are eating. I have operated in many of the hottest deserts on earth and I know all I need to do is keep well hydrated and eat healthy, natural wholefoods with a handful of salted nuts a day and I am fine. If the heat is not extreme, I always eat unsalted nuts. Remember: too *much* salt in your body basically increases the density of your blood, meaning your heart has to work harder to pump it around. That's why high salt equals high blood pressure and a weaker heart.

Scouts aim to live long, healthy lives and that starts with the daily habit of regulating what fuel we put inside our bodies. Be smart. Anyone can be fat and unhealthy and Scouts should aspire to be neither. Set yourself high standards and look after your body. It is your tool for survival, fun and adventure!

BEAR'S SECRET SCOUTING TIPS

If you're worried that you might be losing salt, taste your sweat. If it tastes salty – like tears – you're OK. If not, you need to replace the salt through your diet.

THE APPLICATION OF HEAT

You can survive on cold food. Indeed, in the military we would go for long periods at a time on what was called 'hard routine' – minimal noise, no fires, no cooking, no smoking (if you smoked!), always ready to move and often fast. But a hot meal at the end of the day is going to warm you and cheer you much more than cold rations. The Scouts isn't the military. But if you want to thrive in the wild and work well in a team in order to achieve exceptional feats of service, endurance and adventure, hot, warming food will make that job much easier.

Cooking not only makes most foods more palatable, it destroys dangerous bacteria and toxins. So if you want to eat well *and* safely, you need to know how to cook your food.

Cooking is nothing more than the application of constant and adequate heat. So before we look at the different ways of cooking in the field, we need to think about where that heat's going to come from. Away from the comforts of your own kitchen, you have two choices: trail stoves or a full-blown cooking fire.

| Trail stoves

Trail stoves – the sort of thing people use in holiday campsites the world over – generally use gas or liquid fuel. They can be massively useful in the field. You might find yourself in a location where there's no wood available, or where you're not allowed to light an open fire. Maybe it's cold, and you want to raise your body temperature quickly with a hot drink, or you just need a little hot water to rehydrate some trail food (see pages 106–7). Perhaps the weather conditions are particularly poor, making firelighting difficult. Trail stoves are what I consider an important luxury.

They do have their disadvantages, though. The fuel can be heavy to carry: if you're out in the field for extended periods, the amount of fuel you can take with you will soon run out. It's very difficult to cook for larger numbers on a small trail stove, or to cook food that takes longer than about half an hour. And you're limited in the different cooking methods you can reasonably practise on them.

Don't write them off: they can be seriously valuable bits of kit, but there is a time and a place for when they are best used. You'll be much more competent in the field if you know how to construct an effective cooking fire.

The trail stove: your best friend when you need a warming brew.

Grilling food is one of the speediest ways of getting your
vital fuel cooked and ready to eat.

All fires need nurturing. Look after them when they're small and they'll look after you when they're big.

Cooking fires

In the last chapter we got the lowdown on the theory of fire, the fire triangle and how to light a campfire successfully. For cooking purposes, the criss-cross fire (see page 86) is probably the best choice, as it burns down quickly to a hot, uniform bed.

Cooking should be done over glowing coals, never over flames, which will simply cover your food and utensils in soot as well as scorching the outside of the pan you are using. Once your fire has burned down to glowing coals, you can keep it going by feeding it with small pieces of wood – but never so much that you create large flames.

COOKING METHODS

With a bit of know-how, you can replicate most of the cooking methods you might use in an ordinary kitchen – after all, people have been cooking in the great outdoors for far longer than they have with all mod cons.

Boiling

This is probably the most common method of campfire cooking. In terms of food as fuel, it's the most efficient way of cooking because boiled food

BEAR'S SECRET SCOUTING TIPS

It's a weird fact of physics that the higher up you are the longer water takes to reach sufficient heat to kill parasites and bacteria. Should you find yourself at a very high altitude, don't try and boil water unless you really have to – it takes too long and uses up precious fuel.

maintains most of its vitamins and minerals. If you have to eat meat, boiling it avoids losing all the high-energy fats and other nutrients; but take care not to boil your food for too long, as this will leach it of these essential nutrients. Veggies definitely benefit from the minimum amount of boiling in order to keep the nutrients 'live'.

Most things can be boiled, but you'll probably find it most useful for pasta and rice (brown, wholewheat versions, of course) and vegetables. You will need a container, as well as some means of suspending it over the fire (most trail pots

IMPROVISING IN THE FIELD

In the absence of a suitable pot, it's possible to boil water in a scooped-out log – or any other depression – by dropping heated stones into it. I used this technique recently in a cave in Turkey where I was exploring the ancient Christian hideouts where believers escaped persecution from the Romans. They used to live in a series of impenetrable tunnels and caves dug into the side of vertical cliffs. These caves were almost entirely unexplored and you could see the holes in the ground they used to cook in. One of these was perfect to fill with water and cook the crabs that I had just caught in the river. All I had to do was light a fire (outside the cave, of course), heat some big stones on it and carry them (I was wearing gloves at the time) inside. I then dropped the hot rocks into the small pits filled with water and the crabs were soon cooked through. And I can assure you I wasn't the first person to have done exactly that in those caves.

TRAINING EXERCISES

Being able to bring a pot of water to the boil is a crucial skill that you should practise before you go out in the field. If there are a few of you, you could have a competition. Each person has to collect their own wood and light their own fire. The first person to bring a pint of water to the boil is the winner.

would be damaged if you placed them directly on to the coals of your camp fire). You can construct a simple frame over your fire and suspend your pots from it as shown opposite.

You can also boil water over a fire in a vessel made out of birch bark. Do this over a small fire and it shouldn't burn below the waterline.

Poaching

Poaching is cooking by simmering in a small amount of liquid – somewhere between boiling and steaming. It's a good way of cooking if water is in short supply or if you just want to take the edge off your vegetables. It's also good for eggs and fish. Get a little water simmering in the bottom of a pan, add the

Hunting for crabs in the Turkish mountains. If you know what to look for, the natural world can provide gourmet stuff!

food and keep turning it over for a few minutes. For fish, poach it until it is cooked through and comes away in chunky flakes.

Stewing

Stewing is cooking for a long time in water that has been brought to the boil, then left to simmer below boiling point. It can be a very tasty and nutritious way of cooking, especially for root vegetables to which you can add any number of spices and flavours. Let your imagination be your guide. Scouts should be fervent innovators – especially when cooking! Stewing is also a good way of cooking fruit, although most stewed fruits need brown sugar (or better, and healthier, honey) to make them palatable.

Stewing produces great results, but as it calls for long, slow cooking, careful fire management is crucial and it's not really suitable for trail stoves. Be careful to let your stew simmer – not boil – otherwise it can end up stewed to death and unappetizing.

Frying

Frying – cooking in a pan with a film of natural oil – might sound like the easiest way of preparing food in the field. In fact, it can be very difficult over a campfire because of the difficulty of keeping a constant temperature over a wide enough area. For this reason, frying is more suited to trail-stove cooking; even then it can be difficult to provide enough food for more than a few people using this method. It's also the least healthy option, so keep it for treats, like a Sunday bacon and tomato sandwich (my goodness, I've had a few good ones of those out in the wilds!).

Baking

No one's going to expect you to start knocking up sponge cakes in the field, but baking – cooking food by the application of dry heat in an oven – can be a very effective and efficient way of cooking food in the field.

First, of course, you need an oven. There are several neat ways of making these in the field. The simplest is by using a sheet of tin foil. Wrap a potato in foil and place it in the embers of a fire and it will soon cook through. Alternatively, you could try to make one of the following improvised ovens. Bear in mind the limitations of camp ovens: you can't easily regulate the heat, and only experience will tell you how long your food is likely to take to cook.

Bedouin oven

This is one of the oldest types of field ovens. It can be used for cooking anything from vegetables to entire animals.

Make your oven by digging a hole in the ground between half a metre and a metre deep and as wide as you need, depending on what food you are cooking. Line the floor and the walls of the hole with stones. Light a good fire, then cover the hole with two big, flat stones, taking care to leave a gap at the top so that the air circulates and the fire doesn't go out (don't forget the fire triangle!).

When the flat stones have become very hot, remove them (use gloves!), sweep away the ashes and line the bottom of the oven with leaves or grass on top of the small base stones, making sure you don't use anything that has a particularly strong or unpleasant flavour as this will be imparted into whatever you are cooking.

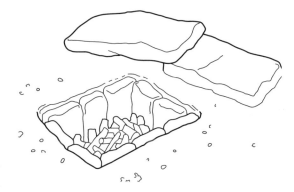

It's now time to add the food. If you're baking a piece of meat that still has the rind, sew it up so that the rind protects the meat; otherwise just place your food in the oven and cover the top with the flat stones. If you're baking vegetables, occasionally pour a little boiling water into the oven to keep the air moist.

A large oven of this kind can stay hot for up to 24 hours.

Maori hangi

This is similar to a Bedouin oven, and is a very popular method of cooking food in the field. The food is wrapped in leaves, then placed on hot stones in a pit and covered with sand or soil. There is no need to add a lid of stones. The food is steamed in its own moisture and comes out very tender.

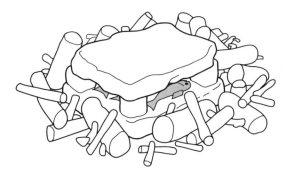

Two-stone oven

This is an excellent way of baking thin slices of meat or flatbreads. Find yourself two large, flat stones and lay them on top of each other with a few smaller stones in between so they are not touching. Make a large fire around the stones so that they become very hot, then slide your food between the stones and let it cook through.

Pot oven

It you have two sturdy cooking pots you can use them to improvise a very fast, hot oven. Place the first pot in the embers of a fire, then put the food you want to cook inside. Cover with the second pot, into which you have put a shovelful of the red-hot embers. Your food will be heated from all sides and should cook quickly.

Beneath a camp fire

An oven of sorts can be improvised simply by digging a hole under your regular campfire, placing the food in the hole and then covering it with earth, embers and fire. Food baked in this way can take many hours to cook, but meat especially will be extremely tender. (You might want to wrap your food in tin foil, if you have it, or some sort of cloth to keep the dirt off.)

| Grilling

This is cooking your food over direct heat. Think barbecue. It's a good method of cooking smaller pieces of meat, fish, chicken, some vegetables like tomatoes or mushrooms, and, of course, for toasting bread. Grilling food requires a bit more attention, because you have to keep turning it, but it's speedier than most other methods of cooking.

There are two main ways of grilling food. The first is by skewering it (a long, green, non-resinous stick that you have sharpened with your knife will do for this) and holding it over the fire. Make sure your skewer is long enough for you not to have to get too close – you don't want to grill yourself as well as the food. Alternatively, you can improvise a grilling rack using long, straight twigs

– green twigs rather than dead ones because they will burn less easily. Make sure they are reasonably thick so that by the time they do start to burn through, your food is cooked. Place a couple of equal-sized logs along either side of your fire and rest the twigs on top. Rest your food at right angles to the twigs and it should cook very quickly.

COOKING UTENSILS, POTS AND PANS

The number and type of pots and pans you take with you on an expedition depends entirely on the nature of the trip. If you're in a fixed camp that can be reached by vehicle, the world's your oyster and you can take a wide range of kettles, urns, pots and frying pans because you know you won't have to carry them on your back. A useful item is a wanigan. This is a waterproof box, originally intended for canoeists, that stores plates, cups, pots, pans, condiments and dried rations.

That said, good meals can be made with surprisingly few pots, but it's important to remember that whatever kit you take with you is kept clean and in good condition. Hygiene is very important, especially when it comes to food, so you need to make sure that cooking equipment doesn't become a danger zone.

As soon as a pot is emptied, fill it with cold water and leave it to soak on or near the fire. If you do this, food remnants will not get the chance to harden and stick to the pan. Wash the pan well with soap and hot water: the soap will dissolve any grease and the hot water will kill any pathogens that might have been attracted to the warm food. (It's a good idea to put a pan of water on for washing up *before* you start to eat, otherwise you could be in for a long wait.) Dry everything carefully to prevent rust.

IMPROVISING IN THE FIELD

If you don't have any soap, damp wood ash is a very good cleaning medium. Just put a little in your pan and use a piece of cloth to scour the food off the sides. (The abrasive qualities of wood ash have been known for a long time – Native Americans used it to clean their teeth! Worth remembering, that one!)

TRAIL FOOD AND CAMP FOOD

The kind of food you're going to eat entirely depends on what you can carry. If you're moving from camp to camp, heavy food and cooking utensils are going to weigh you down; at a fixed camp, however, where you go in by vehicle, you have a lot more scope.

| Trail food

Trail foods need to be lightweight and long lasting. In practice, this means that they tend to be dehydrated or freeze-dried. You can buy all sorts of dried trail foods or army ration packs that simply need rehydrating with the addition of boiling water, but here are three simple recipes that it's good to have up your sleeve, each of which can be made from dried ingredients you can easily carry with you.

Porridge

This not only tastes good, it's also one of the best sources of slow-release energy you can give yourself when you're out in the field. To one quantity of porridge oats, add three quantities of water and a bit of honey. Stir the mixture over a fire until the porridge is cooked to taste. Honey is easy to carry in a small plastic bottle and is great for sweetening all sorts of food – from fruit to stir-frys.

Bread

There are hundreds of recipes for bread, but those that are suitable as trail food are the ones that don't require yeast. This one is easy to remember: just think 3-2-1. Take 3 handfuls of wholewheat flour, 2 handfuls of milk powder and 1 pinch of a raising agent such as cream of tartar or bicarbonate of soda. Mix them together with a little salt and add enough water to form a soft dough. Flatten the dough out into a thin circle. You can cook this bread on a hot, dry frying pan, flipping it over so that it cooks on both sides; or you can bake it in an improvised camp oven (see pages 103–4). Alternatively, you can just put it directly on to the ashes of a dying fire, in which case you will be making what is traditionally called ash cake. Perfect!

Pancakes

You can buy ready-mixed pancake batter, which is less healthy, or you can make your own using wholewheat flour, powdered egg, powdered milk and water. Don't worry too much about proportions – it's not a competition. Use a cupful of flour and a couple of teaspoons each of powdered milk and powdered egg. Whisk in enough water to get the consistency of single cream, then lightly oil a frying pan and pour in enough batter to cover the bottom. Flip it when one side is cooked, then sprinkle with brown sugar or honey and – if you have it in your spice box (see below) – a little cinnamon. It should be delicious.

Trail foods can be bland, but you can spice things up a bit if you take a trail spice box with you. This is just a mini, field-expedient version of your spice rack at home – a small, waterproof box containing plastic containers of, for example, salt, pepper, curry powder, cinnamon, etc. Two plastic bottles, one filled with olive oil, the other with honey, will help you out of many a culinary corner! Remember always to use plastic rather than glass so that the containers don't break.

| Camp food

If you're setting up a fixed base camp for a long time somewhere you can bring supplies in by vehicle, you'll have a lot more choice in terms of what food you can bring with you. Fresh meat and vegetables are more healthy, but you need to be very aware of the fact that there's a limit to how long fresh food will last. You should eat food that's more likely to deteriorate first, leaving the longer-lasting stuff for later in your trip; but there are things you can do to stop your camp food from going off sooner than it otherwise might.

Your camp food needs to be kept somewhere as clean, cool, dry and airy as your situation allows. In a fixed-camp situation, your larder is most likely going to be in a separate tent. Tents can get very warm, so you need to do what you can to keep it cool:

- Pitch your store tent where it will get as much shade as possible.

- If you can't avoid pitching your store tent in direct sunlight, you should move the most perishable foods around the tent as the position of the sun changes throughout the day. Before you go to bed, move the food to the westernmost side of the tent so that it won't be in the way of any early-morning sunlight.

- Open the window flaps of your store tent so a draught can be encouraged. This will substantially reduce the air temperature inside it.

Certain things, like milk and butter, can perish very quickly if they're not kept completely cool. Obviously you won't have electric refrigerators in the field, but I'm going to show you two ways of keeping things cool without the benefit of a bulky white monster!

Cooling in a stream

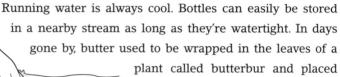

Running water is always cool. Bottles can easily be stored in a nearby stream as long as they're watertight. In days gone by, butter used to be wrapped in the leaves of a plant called butterbur and placed in a stream; nowadays you're more likely to use an airtight container such as a Tupperware box. There's no reason you shouldn't keep meat and fish cool in the same way – just remember to keep different kinds of food in different boxes. Especially, keep raw meat away from foodstuffs that you won't be cooking. If you do use a Tupperware box, either place a rock on top of it, or tie a length of string around the box and then secure it to a rock. Either method will ensure that the box does not get dragged off by the current.

Hayboxes

This is a great way of keeping food cool even when there isn't a stream around. Place your foodstuffs in a sealed box, remembering again to keep raw meat and fish separate. Dig a hole in the ground larger than the volume of the box. Put the box in the hole, then stuff the gaps with hay, dried grass or even newspaper. The stuffing will insulate the box, keeping it cool.

| Unwanted dinner guests

When you're out in the field, you need to be constantly aware that it's not only the humans in your camp that might have a hunger for your food. Ants, flies and even bigger animals will be attracted to the smell of your store tent; and once they start tucking in, at best they can be a nuisance, at worst a real threat to the hygiene and safety of your camp.

Different environments provide different threats in this respect. If you find yourself in bear territory, for example – not unlikely if you ever go trekking in Canada – you should never keep any fresh or strong-smelling food within

100 metres of the camp. Even then you should keep it stored in a sealed plastic bag well up a tree if you don't want it to be swiped by a ravenous grizzly. Bears have been known to break into tents where food is being kept, so in such terrains you should *never* sleep in the same tent as your food. I have one friend who went to sleep in his tent with an apple in his pocket and woke when a bear had torn its way into the tent and was madly ripping at his trousers in an attempt to get the fruit! He was lucky to survive.

Even if you're not in bear country, the smell of food is like a beacon for unwanted animals. For this reason, you should always do the following:

- If you have any meat, cover it with a fine mesh netting, making sure there is an air gap between the meat and the netting so that flies cannot land on it. Flies eat by vomiting a mixture of digestive juices that dissolve their food; they then suck it back up again. Not really what you want to happen to your dinner, right? They can also spread diseases such as cholera, typhoid and dysentery. And if flies land on your meat it can get 'flyblown', when they lay their eggs on it and then maggots hatch out. You can buy nets that make this job easier, but you can improvise by using a piece of mosquito netting.

- Fruit and vegetables kept in plastic bags will sweat and go rotten faster. Keep them open in a cool, airy place and check them regularly for any that look like they're on the turn – they'll be a magnet for creepy crawlies – and dispose of them carefully.

- Keep the floor of your camp store scrupulously clean. If it has a canvas floor, sweep it regularly; if not, rake or scrape the earth away. The tiniest crumb can attract a legion of ants.

- Dispose of your rubbish carefully. It might look like garbage to you, but to insects and animals it's a free meal. Either burn it, or keep it in sealed bags well away from the food area. Get rid of it responsibly. You're a Scout and a force for good: part of your role is looking after our Earth and not filling it with trash.

WATER

You can go without food for much longer than you think – up to several weeks, in fact – but without water, you're brown bread: dead. Our bodies are 70 per cent water and it's essential for almost all our bodily functions. Under normal circumstances, we excrete more than 3 litres of water a day – two from our kidneys and one from our skin as sweat. Heat, cold, exercise and altitude – all of which you are likely to experience in the field – cause our bodies to expel even more water, and it has to be replaced.

Without water, our blood turns to sludge and becomes less effective at performing its vital work of taking oxygen to our muscles. As we become dehydrated, we start experiencing certain symptoms: thirst, obviously, but also nausea, dizziness and lack of energy. Our urine becomes dark brown and smells bad, our skin becomes less elastic and we become very tired. Whatever you do, don't ignore these signs. If your body's saying you need water, you're already dehydrated. The key to staying hydrated is to drink *before* you need to. If you lose just 15 per cent of your body's fluids, you die. But even if you lose just a fraction of that amount, your performance and ability to act and think at your peak is seriously reduced. Scouts can't afford to lose that vital edge. Letting yourself become severely dehydrated is a lesson you tend to learn just once. You end up hopeless and powerless.

I remember very well what happened to one fellow recruit going through the French Foreign Legion's simulated basic training with me. We were in the Western Sahara in the old Legion fort on another sweltering desert day of back-breaking hard labour and brutal exercise. The recruit had lost a glove on a long night route march. His punishment was to wear all – and I mean *all* – his equipment and clothing for the whole of the following day. This meant two thick woolly jerseys over two shirts over two T-shirts, two hats, gloves, two pairs of trousers, a jacket, his rucksack, three pairs of socks (two of them worn as gloves over his other gloves!) and his thermals. Needless to say, he had soon sweated more than he could drink in fluids, and collapsed. He looked like a ghost and had to lie in bed on a drip for two days while he recovered.

That's an extreme example, but it didn't take long for him to drop, despite his great fitness and stamina. Whatever activities you're doing, you need to keep hydrated. Don't be the one who gets caught out. And just because you're not in the Sahara doesn't mean you don't need to drink. You can lose almost as much in cold climates as you do in hot, the added danger being that people assume that because it's cold, they don't need to drink much water. They are very wrong. In cold environments you pee more as your body expels waste fluids on which it doesn't want to waste energy keeping warm.

As I mentioned before the golden rule is to drink water *before* you get thirsty. And don't be tempted to hydrate by drinking fizzy pop or supposed 'energy' drinks. On the whole these are packed with bad sugars that only serve to make you thirsty and fat! I call them empty calories. Stick to water to hydrate and enjoy those other drinks for what they are – the odd treat around a campfire.

Ultimately, to keep hydrated you first need to find water then, just as importantly, you need to make it drinkable.

| Finding water

The most obvious sources of water are streams and lakes. If you have these nearby, then water won't be a problem *as long as you purify it* (see pages 112–14). In the right weather you can collect rainwater, which as long as it goes into a clean vessel, will generally be safe to drink without purifying.

But what if you don't have the benefit of a water source or a full rain cloud? The good news is that water exists in even the most arid environments – you just have to know how to get your hands on it. If you think about it, it makes sense: all forms of life, including plants, need water to survive. So if you see greenery, there's water somewhere. Here are two ways of collecting it.

Above-ground solar still

Making a solar still relies on the principle of condensation. When you have a shower at home, the warm water vapour hits a cold window or mirror and turns back into liquid water. Solar stills do the same thing, only the window is a plastic bag and the shower-head is a plant.

To make a solar still, you need some green, non-poisonous vegetation. Fill a clear plastic bag about three-quarters full with the vegetation, then tie the mouth of the bag tightly. Put the bag in direct sunlight. As the plant photosynthesizes (the process of turning carbon dioxide into oxygen and water) the leaves will give off water vapour. As the water vapour hits the plastic bag, it reverts to liquid water, which you can then collect. Set up several of these stills, though, as you don't get much water from each one.

Below-ground solar still

A below-ground still also uses the principle of condensation and is a good way of extracting water from ground that you know contains moisture.

BEAR'S SECRET SCOUTING TIPS

To get more water from a below-ground solar still, line the hole with green, non-poisonous vegetation. If you do this, you might need to dig a slightly bigger hole; but as you're mixing the techniques used by both solar stills, you should get considerably more water. You can also pee into the earth around the container to make the still as damp as possible. The process of condensation will turn the moisture in your urine into clean drinking water.

Dig a hole about a metre across and 60cm deep. Place a clean container at the bottom of the hole, making an indentation to keep it upright. If you have a length of tubing, place one end in the container and the other outside the hole so you can drink the water you collect without having to disturb the still.

Lay a piece of plastic sheeting over the hole, covering the edge with rocks, soil or sand to keep it in place. Now place a rock in the centre of the plastic.

You want the plastic to be about 40cm below ground level and for the rock to be directly above the container. Moisture from the earth will condense on the bottom of the plastic sheet and drip directly into your container. Again, several stills will give you more water.

| Purifying water

Before we talk about *how* to purify water, let's look at *why*. Water can look clear, pure and delicious; but that doesn't mean it's not harbouring some extremely nasty things. Water-borne illnesses like cholera and typhoid can both kill; dysentery is characterized by bad diarrhoea, bloody pooh, a high fever and can lead to extreme dehydration; flukes are a kind of parasitic worm that can be found in stagnant, polluted water – they live as parasites in your bloodstream and cause disease. These illnesses are some of the most vicious you can contract in the field. I have suffered several times in the wild from drinking dodgy water, through a mixture of bad luck and sometimes plain, simple error. However fit and strong you are, if you're

hit by dysentery you're pretty useless and become a dead weight to those around you.

One of my best friends was out hiking in the Welsh mountains, training for Special Forces selection. He innocently drank from a clear mountain stream, not knowing there was a dead sheep a hundred metres higher up the mountain. He contracted a terrifying illness that meant he could no longer attempt selection and which gave him chronic fatigue for two years. Always remember that a bad decision has an implication, a ripple. So learn from the mistakes of others and keep healthy so you can continue being an effective Scout.

Fortunately, purifying clear water is easy. You can buy water purification tablets that will quickly make it drinkable. These are made of chlorine or iodine: both make the water taste a bit funny, but you can buy neutralizing tablets to get rid of that taste.

In an emergency you can boil water in a plastic bottle. It's weird but it works, as the water stops the plastic from melting.

Alternatively, you can purify water by boiling it. At sea level, boiling for one minute will be enough; for each additional 300 metres you are above sea level, boil for an extra minute. (If you're not sure how high up you are, 10 minutes will always be enough.)

| Filtering water

If your water is cloudy, muddy, stagnant or smells foul then you will have to filter it before you purify it. An improvised water filter is easy to make using a cloth bag and some string. Tie the stitched end tightly with string. Then fill it with layers of filtering material with the least coarse material at the bottom: put in some fine sand first, add some small stones and then some large stones at the top. If you also include bits of charcoal from your fire, this will absorb some toxins and bad smells from the water. Make a couple of small holes in the open end and attach a piece of string so you can hang it from a tree branch.

BEAR'S SECRET SCOUTING TIPS

Purified water should be kept in dark containers or under cover, as ultra-violet rays from the sun can neutralize the effects of your purifying agents.

HIDDEN DANGERS

Remember that these methods for filtering and purifying are only good for fresh water, not salt water.

Pour your cloudy water into the bag and let it drip through into a clean container. *Remember that you still have to purify water that has been filtered before you drink it.*

| Carrying water

There are a couple of ways of carrying water in the field; each comes with its advantages and disadvantages.

Water bottles

Bottles are convenient, easy to get hold of and very useful (for carrying water as well as for other jobs). If you are going to carry your water in a bottle, however – and most people do – you need to know some simple biology. The body can only absorb about a pint of water an hour. If you drink it at a faster rate than this, you will simply pee the excess away. Not only is this a waste of a precious resource, it can also lull you into a false sense of security. It is easy to assume, because you have drunk two pints, that you must be well hydrated, and drinking more water than your body can absorb will make your pee look deceptively clear.

The trouble with bottles is that they encourage you to drink faster than you should. It's a palaver to stop, remove your backpack and find your water bottle; so you're likely to gulp large quantities less frequently, rather than take small, regular sips. Drink too much too quickly and you won't get the benefit; so if you carry water in a bottle, take care to regulate your intake.

IMPROVISING IN THE FIELD

If you need to filter water in an emergency and don't have a cloth bag, you can cut off a trouser leg or use a sock. See pages 64–6 for the lowdown on making natural cordage to hang up the bag with, too.

Camelbaks

A camelbak is a pouch that goes over your back or your rucksack, with a plastic tube that you drink through. It means you can take small sips whenever you want to, without having to go through the rigmarole of finding your bottle. It sounds like a small thing, but the advent of camelbaks has drastically reduced the incidence of heat exhaustion in the military – stopping to take water from your pack is extremely perilous when you're under fire.

The only downside of a camelbak is that it must be cleaned regularly with a mild disinfectant, such as Milton fluid, otherwise bacteria can build up from any stagnant water left inside.

EMERGENCY RATIONS

If you're living wild, you need to be prepared for food to run out. If that happens, you'll be glad to have squirreled away some emergency rations. These need to be very high in slow-release energy. Over the years, Scouts and fieldcraft experts have developed two miracle foodstuffs called pemmican and pinole. They last almost indefinitely – certainly for many years – they have a high concentration of energy for their weight; they're easy to make; and they require no cooking when you want to eat them. You can survive entirely on either one for long periods of time.

Pemmican

Properly made, this provides almost every nutrient you need with the exception of vitamin C. During the Second Boer War, British soldiers were given an emergency ration of 4 ounces of pemmican and 4 ounces of chocolate or sugar. These rations were attached to the soldiers' belts in small iron tins – the origin of the phrase 'iron rations'. A soldier was supposed to be able to march for 36 hours on these iron rations.

To make pemmican, you need equal quantities of shredded dried meat and suet. Grind the dried meat to a powder, then melt the suet and mix them so you get a consistency like sausage meat. Keep it in a watertight container.

I have some friends who travelled to the South Pole, replicating Captain Scott's fateful expedition. They lived as he lived, eating pemmican. It tastes like hell and is not a healthy way to live for long, but there is no denying its credentials as a long-lasting, calorific, high-energy food. But only use it if you have no alternative, or you'll hate me!

Pinole

Pinole is far better tasting and healthier than pemmican and is made by drying corn kernels. You can do this in an oven or, if you're out in the field, in the ashes of your fire. The brown kernels can be eaten as they are, or ground to a powder. A handful of pinole powder in a cup of cold water can keep you going for several hours. (You can also make a version of pinole from the dried seeds of most grasses, but they won't be as nutritious as corn.)

These days there are items you can buy to save going through the rigmarole of making pemmican and pinole. Look for all-natural granola bars, which are your pinole; and 'gorp' or trail mix (a mixture of dried fruit, raisins, nuts or similar), which are your pemmican/iron rations.

Now you're all set! You know how to stay healthy and hydrated and, more importantly, how to stay that way while you're in the field. So go get 'em!

Real-life campfire story

For centuries food has been the cause of riots, unrest and mutinies the world over, yet it is something we often give little thought to until we are hungry. As rations become low, performance drops off rapidly, energy levels suffer and morale takes a nosedive. It is therefore very important that rationing is planned well in advance of any trip into the field, whether it is for a small party of friends going camping or a Scout jamboree. Get the food right, keep the troops happy and the remainder will follow.

We have talked in this chapter about how much more energy our bodies require when we are exerting ourselves. A friend of mine found this out to his peril on a particularly gruelling operation. Special Forces soldiers are required to carry extremely large quantities of specialist equipment, ammunition and stores in their packs in order to fulfil their missions, often without resupply. On this occasion they were weighing every last ounce of food and equipment to make sure each soldier had enough and that it was distributed equally between them.

Unfortunately for my friend, the amount of equipment and ammunition that he had to carry meant that something had to be forfeited. The only option was the food. Not all of it, but some. The rations were broken down and he went through each day, laying out what he thought he could survive on, giving himself a little treat of a bar of chocolate every third day, but keeping the remainder to the bare minimum so that he could get his pack on to his back and still operate effectively. There were to be no Cordon Bleu cooking experiences on this trip!

The patrol deployed and the first few days weren't too bad. It soon became apparent, however, that he had underestimated the amount of food he would need. At the end of each day he felt weaker and he was very aware of his faculties becoming increasingly less acute. Afraid that he would let his patrol members and himself down, he took the decision to break into his next day's rations, telling himself that he still had his bars of chocolate in reserve if things became desperate.

The days marched on and so did the patrol; the hunger pangs struck deeper and deeper and he delved a little more into the next day's rations, until eventually he was eating food meant for two days ahead. Things were not looking good and although he knew the expected duration of the mission, there was always the possibility that it could get extended on task or that pick-up could be delayed. He just hoped that he could hold out, but knew it wasn't going to be easy. Eventually he had to give in, and the chocolate that had been put aside as a treat had now become an emergency ration. There were no more true rations.

Fortunately for him, this was a training mission. The patrol did come to an end as expected and there were no delays as there often are (both on a military operation and on a trek). The patrol was extracted having completed a successful mission, but he ended up sitting on the extraction helicopter sharing a sachet of sugar from a brew kit with a friend – their remaining rations for that day!

The moral of the story is this: plan and plan well. Never underestimate the amount of food you will need – and then add some. At the end of the day if you have too much you can always give it away – or better still you can eat it. But if push comes to shove, you can always call on my friend – since that event he has always got plenty of spare rations on him! A lesson learned the hard way.

Chapter 6

LIVING WILD

best practices and techniques when living in the field

Many people think that living out of doors is in some way less civilized than living at home. This isn't true – at least, it shouldn't be. Getting away from amenities such as mains water and on-tap entertainment is incredibly liberating; but it doesn't mean that the benefits of these amenities should be forgotten about. When you're living with other people in the field, it doesn't mean you've removed yourself from society. It just means you've joined a different kind of society and the wild outdoors is now your playground.

All societies have rules and regulations; ways of making sure that the individual looks after him or herself and the group to the benefit of all. In this chapter we're going to look at ways of making sure that your time in the field is as happy, healthy and productive as it should be.

PERSONAL HYGIENE

The word 'hygiene' comes from Hygieia, who was the Greek goddess of health. It's worth remembering that. Good hygiene isn't just a luxury: it's essential for good health. If you're living in a fixed camp, it can have a bad effect on everyone if a single person falls ill. And as you might be living in close proximity to other people, illness and disease can spread quickly and with catastrophic effects; just ask any soldier who's been stationed in a hot climate and been struck down with the dreaded D & V – diarrhoea and vomiting. Once one person goes down with it, so can the rest of the camp. It makes for a pretty miserable time.

It's a common misapprehension that living wild is inherently unhygienic. It might at times be a bit muddier than normal (as a kid I always wanted to be muddy – and I still do, if truth be told); but muddy is different from unhygienic. In fact, living wild is no more unhygienic than living at home, but it does present you with different hygiene issues. In order to keep healthy in the field, you should divide your hygiene routine into three parts: body, feet and teeth.

Body

In terms of cleanliness, moisture is not your friend. The parts of your body that are prone to dampness – your armpits, crotch, feet and hair – are prone to infestation and infection. You should wash these areas thoroughly every day if you can. Take care to clean under your fingernails, where a lot of harmful bacteria can lurk. If you have a problem finding water to wash in,

IMPROVISING IN THE FIELD

The white ashes from your fire can be used as a soap substitute, as can sand and loamy soil. Mix white ash with melted animal fat to improvise a field soap bar.

you should remove as many clothes as you can and let the air get to your skin so that it dries out any moist areas. If you can do this in the sunshine, then so much the better. Sunlight has great antibacterial qualities – but just make sure you don't get burned.

When you're hiking, your clothes will absorb sweat and may become damp. Damp clothes can be as unhygienic as damp skin, so try to dry them out – again in direct sunlight if possible – whenever it's convenient. The same goes for sleeping bags, sheets and blankets. They should be aired as much as possible during the day. If the weather's nice, try draping your sleeping bag over the roof of your tent for an hour in the morning. (But don't leave it there and go away, or you may find it's blown off and is lying in a stream – I've seen that happen!)

Dry out sweaty or wet clothes whenever you can.
Remember the sun also kills bacteria.

| Feet

With sore feet, you're not going anywhere – at least not comfortably. If you neglect them, you'll have a seriously miserable time. You can't avoid getting sweaty feet, and when you're hiking you often can't avoid getting your boots wet. Having the proper gear and knowing how to look after it (see Chapter 1) will be a great help. But you should wash and – crucially – dry your feet at regular intervals to stop them becoming cracked, damaged and infected.

Blisters are the bane of any keen hiker. Well-fitting boots will go a long way to preventing them. Wearing a thin pair of synthetic inner socks will draw any moisture from your feet and will reduce friction against the skin; both factors

Keeping your feet dry will help prevent
blisters – the bane of any hiker.

TRAINING EXERCISES

Sometimes blisters are unavoidable. But you can train your feet to be more resistant to them by making the skin tougher. Try rubbing them in methylated spirit before setting out on a hike. Of course, you can do this any time, not just when you're in the field. I used to do this a lot during my military service as a way of toughening my feet against blisters.

IMPROVISING IN THE FIELD

If you feel a blister coming on when you are out in the field, you can sometimes stop it developing by placing a piece of cool moss on the inside of your sock. Just make sure it doesn't increase the pressure on the sore patch.

that will help avoid blisters. But if you do feel a blister coming on – the telltale 'hot spot' – stop walking, remove your boots and socks, then dry and air your feet.

If you do get a blister, don't be tempted to burst it. The moisture of a blister is your body's way of cushioning the sore patch; if you burst it, it will become prone to infection. If it bursts naturally, treat it as you would any other wound (see pages 206–7).

Remember that feet like to breathe. When you're in camp, wear flip-flops or sandals whenever possible. It's much healthier than encasing them in leather coffins!

| Teeth

When you set out on a field trip don't forget your toothbrush! But if you *do* find yourself in the field without one, you can make an improvised version. Find a sturdy twig, such as hazel or alder, and chew on the end so the fibres

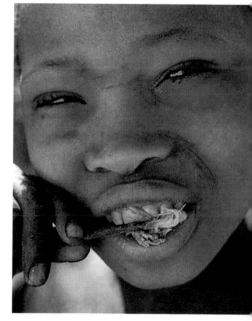

Nature can provide most of the things that chemists can!

separate and become brush-like, then use this to clean your teeth and gums. Remember only to use purified water to clean your teeth (see pages 112–14).

A box of dental floss weighs almost nothing – especially if you remove the floss from its plastic case – but using it every day can make a big difference. My dentist says it is more important even than brushing, so take note. Fellow climbers always used to tease me about endlessly flossing halfway up a mountain, but they're the ones with mouths full of fillings now!

GROUP HYGIENE

Everyone is individually responsible for their own personal hygiene, but at a fixed camp, group hygiene is everyone's responsibility.

| Rubbish

When you pitch camp, you need to designate an area for non-human waste, of which there are three types: kitchen grease, biodegradable waste and non-biodegradable waste.

Kitchen grease

Greasy water will attract flies and insects, and you can build a grease trap in the following way. Dig a pit, then find some long, straight sticks that you can weave together in a criss-cross pattern (see diagram). Weave some long grass or broad leaves into the wooden framework and then place this over the pit. You can now pour greasy water on to it: the leaves will catch the grease and can then be burned and replaced, while the water will drain away.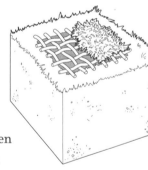

Biodegradable waste

This will mainly consist of kitchen peelings and solid cooking grease. The good news is that you can get rid of biodegradable waste easily and do the environment a favour at the same time. Dig a slops pit – deep so that it doesn't attract vermin and at a good distance from the camp – and pour your biodegradable waste into it. When you leave, cover it with soil. The slops will compost naturally, and you'll have given something back to the land. (This may not be possible at a public site; bag this waste up and take it away with you when you leave.)

Non-biodegradable waste

Generally speaking, this will be anything man-made and you'll have to take it away with you when you leave camp. Tin cans should be topped and tailed so that they squash down easily, then burned in the fire to get rid of any food residue and stop them being a magnet for insects, mice and rats. Torch batteries should never be thrown on the fire. Take them off camp and dispose of them correctly.

Remember, you're only borrowing your campsite. Imagine you are the next people to use it. You should leave it as litter-free as you found it.

Washing facilities

If there's a decent-sized stream nearby, then you have nature's own bath and sink rolled into one – just make sure you use a biodegradable soap. If you don't have one, you will need to improvise (see page 123).

Camp washstand

At a fixed camp, it might be worth setting up a camp washstand. You can see how to make a simple washstand on page 75, but for longer-term fixed camps this is a more hygienic method because it allows the water to run away into a soakaway pit.

You'll need six lengths of wood, each about a metre long and three of which should have forked ends, a bowl, a piece of tarp and some cordage. Make a frame for the washstand as shown so that the tarp can be folded and tied along its length to form a funnel for drainage. Dig a hole where the water will drain out so that you don't get a soggy, messy patch of ground. The bowl can be attached to the frame by making a 'cradle' of cordage underneath it.

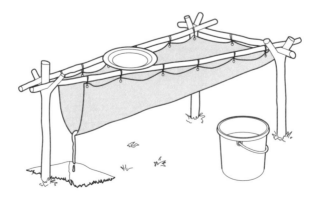

Camp shower

A fixed-camp shower can be improvised in a couple of ways. Tie a rope to the handle of a watering can and loop the rope over the

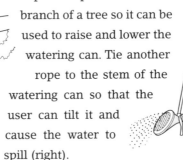

branch of a tree so it can be used to raise and lower the watering can. Tie another rope to the stem of the watering can so that the user can tilt it and cause the water to spill (right).

Alternatively, make a small hole in a bucket. Then attach a tube with a watering can rose at one end and fit the other end into the hole. Fill the bucket with water and suspend it from a branch. The shower can be turned 'on' and 'off' by draping the pipe back into the bucket (left).

FIELD SANITATION

In the American army, recruits are taught the five Fs of field sanitation: fingers, flies, foods, fluids and faeces. These are the principle means by which infection can be transmitted. We've already dealt with fingers, flies, foods and fluids. Which just leaves faeces!

Now, one thing I know for certain is that everyone, even the Queen of England, needs to use the loo. If you're on the trail, you should just dig a small hole, answer nature's call and then cover it over. This is also a reasonable way of doing things at a short-term camp where there aren't many people. But at a longer-term fixed camp where there are a lot of people producing a lot of waste, good sanitation is crucial. Faeces are the principal means by which organisms that cause intestinal disease are transmitted, so you need to make sure they are dealt with properly. This means digging your own latrine. In fact, this should be one of the first jobs you think about. There are three things to consider when building a camp latrine: location, construction and maintenance.

Location

No matter how good your field sanitation, you can't get away from the fact that there's going to be a certain amount of odour coming from your latrine. For this reason, you should build it at a good distance from the living quarters of your fixed camp and on the leeward side so that the wind does not blow the smell back towards you. If you're camping on a slope, the latrine should be built below the camp so that drainage doesn't flow back towards it; and it should be built well away from any water sources. If you can, build your latrine where users will get some sort of natural privacy, and it's always better built in the shade so that direct sunlight doesn't make it smell worse.

Construction

A camp latrine should consist of a 'wet' and a 'dry' pit: one for urine, one for faeces.

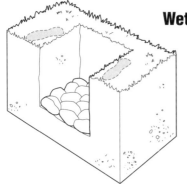

Wet pit

This should be about 50cm square and 50cm deep. Line the bottom with stones so that you get a soakaway rather than a smelly, muddy pit. Boys can just stand and aim; girls, I'm afraid you'll have to squat!

Dry pit

Your dry pit should be about 90cm long, 30cm wide and 60cm deep. When you dig your hole, make sure you pile the displaced earth at one side of the pit. After you've been, you can shovel a small pile of earth on top, which will stop it smelling (and looking!) so bad.

For the sake of privacy, you can erect a four-pole screen around your latrine. The front flap should be loose so that it serves as a door, but with a piece of wood tied along the bottom so that it doesn't blow open in windy weather.

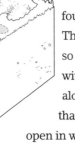

It is possible to build latrine seats. However, you need to be pretty confident in your woodcraft skills to do this, as it's really not the sort of thing you want to collapse beneath you! Better just to straddle and squat, which is good for the thigh muscles too.

Maintenance

The wet pit will take care of itself. The dry pit needs proper management. It is essential to put a shovelful of the displaced earth over the pit each time it's used. You should only use biodegradable loo roll in the field, which should be kept in your tent rather than by the latrine to stop it getting wet.

It might be tempting to pour antibacterial products into your latrine. Don't. These will kill the beneficial bacteria in the soil, and stop the latrine from composting naturally. When it comes to within 15cm of the top, fill it in again with what remains of the displaced earth and build a new latrine.

When you've finished using the latrine, don't forget to wash your hands (remember that fingers are one of the five Fs). In the military, they often use alcohol gel: you just rub this into your hands and leave it to dry. It's readily available, and it's a very useful and sanitary product.

KEEPING CLEAN ON THE TRAIL

Sometimes it's just not practical to dig latrines and construct elaborate washing facilities. If you're not making a fixed camp, or are just hiking from day to day, your hygiene arrangements are going to be smaller in scale. This, however, doesn't mean they should be neglected.

Obviously, if you're near a stream, keeping clean is more straightforward than if your supply of water is limited. It's amazing how much dirt you can remove, however, using just a little of your trail water. Before you set off, cut the bottom from a plastic milk bottle. It weighs almost nothing in your pack, but makes a very useful – if small – portable sink. A bit of cloth, or better still a small sponge (again, this weighs almost nothing), and you have the means to wash easily and make efficient use of your water supply.

I have already suggested using alcohol gel to clean your hands in a fixed camp. On the trail it can be put to even wider use, disinfecting all those areas of the body where bacteria can accumulate, especially armpits, crotch and feet. A few drops of alcohol gel on cotton wool balls is a great way of keeping clean

BEAR'S SECRET SCOUTING TIPS

If you use alcohol gel and cotton wool to keep clean, don't throw the cotton wool balls away. Doused with the alcohol gel, they make very effective tinder for firelighting.

where water is scarce and facilities are limited. Wet wipes or baby wipes are another good alternative as they require no water and can be burned when you want to get rid of them.

Trail sanitation is a lot less elaborate than fixed-camp sanitation, but the principle is the same. Take a small trowel with you and, when nature calls, dig a hole. Make sure it's well covered up when you've finished. If you're burying toilet roll, make sure it's biodegradable. And don't forget the five Fs – wash your hands when you've finished if you want to avoid unpleasant intestinal infections (again, alcohol gel is invaluable for this).

CAMP ROUTINE AND TEAMWORK

Whether you're at a fixed camp with a large number of people, or there are only a few of you, teamwork matters. I have spent a lot of time in my life operating in hostile environments with small teams of people. The greatest quality I have learned to look for in those I choose to go with is kindness. No one wants to be with a selfish person for long periods of time. Humour is important, as is humility, but nothing ranks higher than being the sort of person who gives your buddy the first cup of tea when you've made a brew, or who shares his snack or helps someone put up a tent. Kindness is a great scouting quality. Show it yourself, value it and encourage it. Remember – there is no I in TEAM.

When there's a large group of you, it's unavoidable that cliques will form. That's human nature, and there's nothing you can do about it. What you *can* do, however, is try to be kind, generous, fun and humble. You'll find that everyone wants to be your friend and morale will be up when people are with you. As any military commander knows, the morale of your men is one of the most important factors in the success of a campaign. Allow morale to fall, and the battle is almost lost. The Royal Marines often talk of 'cheerfulness under adversity', and this is indeed a great quality to show in a group.

An important part of keeping camp morale high is ensuring that every member of that camp has a role, a job to oversee and to take pride in. People like to be given a task to do as it makes them feel empowered. Everyone should have their own individual area of responsibility. This is a simple way of keeping standards up and ensuring that everyone does their bit. I remember one military commander wrote, 'Morale is when a soldier thinks that his army is the best in the world, his regiment the best in the army, his company the best in the regiment, his squad the best in the company and that he himself is the best damned soldier in the outfit.' This kind of pride is good. If you set a high standard for people they will want to live up to it.

Leadership

If you are a leader then remember that good leadership is about leading by example. Never expect others to do what you are not prepared to do yourself. The job of a leader involves going that extra mile to ensure people under your care are safe and well looked after. Remember that people's needs go beyond the physical, so look out for their emotions and sensitivities. A good way to remember this is always to put yourself in other people's shoes.

As leader you will often end up being the last to bed, the first up and the hardest worker, but people will notice this, respond to it and will follow your example. Leadership is NOT an excuse to get others to do the hard work! Good leaders, above all, make you feel special and that you matter. Go at the pace of the slowest and encourage much more than you criticize. Remember to praise in public, and correct in private. Make it fun to be with you and give people the power to make a difference. Leaders encourage others to be great.

Camp rota

In the field, everyone needs to do their bit – to share both the work and the play – otherwise resentments and frustrations can arise. 'The Devil makes work for idle hands' is a very true expression! The best way of ensuring this doesn't happen is through the use of a camp rota.

Members of a camp should be divided into groups. The size of each group will depend on how many people you have at the camp. If the group is too small, the tasks will be accordingly more difficult; likewise, if the group is too large, it becomes easier for those less inclined to work hard to slip away once a couple of small jobs have been completed. Between five and eight is a good number to avoid both these problems. Each group should contain a mixture of ages, personalities and experience in the field. This allows people to mix with the sort of people they might not otherwise get to know.

Once a camp has been set up, the main duties are preparation of food, fetching of water and collection of wood, though this will of course change according to the different requirements the location of your camp presents. The rota should be set up as soon as the camp is in place so everyone knows what is required of them and when.

Camp routine

Routine might sound boring, but in certain situations it's very important. I'm not going to tell you exactly how a camp routine should be set up because it depends on what kind of camp you are in, but there are a few things you should consider when you're deciding how a day in camp should be divided up.

It's important that time is put aside for the important jobs that need doing in a camp. However, it's just as important that there's plenty of time for both group activities and for people to have their own personal quiet time as this means they're more likely to be motivated to give time to the group. I think it's good to spend an hour after breakfast doing the campcraft required for the day.

Food glorious food

Preparing food for a camp full of hungry people is the biggest job of the day. Whichever group is on the food rota should start preparations early if they want to avoid grumbles (and rumbles) later on.

Washing up

No one likes this much, but as we've already seen it's essential to camp hygiene: leaving dirty plates and cooking pans around the camp is the quickest way of attracting flies and other unwanted guests. Either assign the washing up to one group on the rota, or make sure everyone cleans their own plates and cutlery. Whoever's in charge of food preparation should put pots of water on to the fire as soon as the cooking pots are taken off, so there's hot water ready for washing up when you need it.

Inspection

In the army new recruits need to be prepared for an inspection of their kit at any time. There's good reason for this: in a combat situation, troops need to be ready for anything. With their weapons cleaned and their kit

With good teamwork even the mundane can be made fun!

properly squared, they're as ready as they can be for whatever their hostile environment throws at them. Just as importantly, tidiness and cleanliness minimize the likelihood of problems caused by bad hygiene.

When you're in the field, you can learn a lot from the army way of doing things. Part of your daily routine should include airing your tent and your bedclothes and organizing your kit. We've seen that the dampness caused by sweating in bed can lead to poor hygiene. You can't avoid sweating in bed, so you should try and hang your bedclothes out to dry on a daily basis, as well as making sure that the interior of your tent is clean and your rucksack is neatly packed. A morning inspection is a good way of ensuring that the health and comfort of the group isn't compromised by someone ignoring the basics. You can easily make this fun by having rewards for the tidiest tent or the best turned-out Scout.

Teamwork training exercises

Military training focuses heavily on teamwork and you can see why. On the battlefield, when each man is relying not only on his own skills to keep him alive, but also on those of the people around him, the importance of teamwork takes on a different dimension. In survival situations too, teamwork is of the essence.

I have had my life saved on high mountains before and I have, in return, helped save others. In my experience good teamwork boils down to a few simple things: being a friend to people when it matters, being honest and sharing your vulnerabilities with others. None of us is an island; we all need each other from time to time and showing that intimacy is a great way of building strong bonds with others. Everyone likes to help and everyone responds when they feel needed. A team where people can be open and honest, without the fear of anyone laughing at them, is a great team. I have been part of such teams many times on high mountains and in small Special Forces patrols, and being a part of a team like that is what draws me to such environments. It is not about the danger, the adrenalin or the fear; it is about sharing those moments with people you are close to. That's the real magic. Tough places create strong bonds, and where there are bonds, there is strength.

Teamwork doesn't always come naturally to people, especially if they're a bit shy, but everyone benefits from it when it works well, so sometimes you have to practise it. Team-building training exercises don't have to be arduous, however. Think of them as games. Team sports are a good way of building up the sense of shared responsibility that is crucial in the field, but there are other games that help you practise field-expedient skills such as first aid, navigation and firelighting. Here are three such games.

Aeroplane crash

Divide yourselves into four groups of about five people. Pretend that one member of the group is a parachutist who has just escaped from an air crash. Administer first aid for burns and a broken ankle. Make a small fire and boil some water for the patient to drink, and construct a shelter to protect the patient from whatever the prevailing weather conditions are.

Pioneers

Divide yourselves into groups. Each group must imagine they find themselves deep in enemy territory. You need to choose a suitable, well-sheltered site to build a fire and cook some food. You only have a limited amount of time to do this, however. Towards the end of the allowed time, a noise is heard. Enemy soldiers are approaching. Each group needs to strike camp, quickly, leaving no trace that would allow the enemy to work out that they had been there. When the camps have been struck, each group can scour the area to see if they can work out where the others have been.

Triage

This is a good team-building exercise, and also helps you learn the vital skills of basic triage (see page 200). Two of your team go and hide, then act out certain injuries. The rest of the team have to find them, judge the severity of their injuries and administer first aid to stop them 'dying'.

Real-life campfire story

I'll never forget my first ever army training exercise. I was a young, inexperienced recruit, wandering around Salisbury Plain – a vast, open wilderness in southern England – on a freezing cold, wet winter's night. Our patrol was lost. As our enthusiasm shrivelled like our wet fingers, we eventually decided enough was enough. It was time to get some rest. We hadn't slept for a while; our feet were sore and our spirits damp. Sound familiar? I figured there was no point getting into a sleeping bag, I was soaking wet and there was only an hour to go until dawn, so instead I curled up into a ball on my roll mat in the rain, my rifle next to me, and dragged my poncho across my body.

The recruit I was paired up with, however, decided that the likelihood of the 'enemy' finding us in this dank, dark wood was minimal. Despite what we had been told, he stripped off, removed his boots and went head first down his sleeping bag in an attempt to get warm and shut out the miseries of the past 24 hours.

And then, of course, the inevitable happened – we were compromised. Just as I had dozed off, all hell broke loose. The directing staff, acting as the enemy, overran our camp. Flash-bang grenades were going off, blank rounds were fired left, right and centre, there was screaming and shouting and chaos all around. I grabbed my rifle and rucksack, gathered my poncho in my arms and ran in what I had been told was a bomb-burst pattern just to get the hell out of the compromise. As I turned round, I remember seeing this poor recruit running around with no boots, his head still stuffed down his sleeping bag. He looked like a giant, green, panicking worm as he desperately tried to untangle himself. It was a great sight, and one that I have often remembered when it's been cold and wet and I've been trying to sort my kit out in a neat, organized way, ready to move off in a hurry if need be.

These skills come with time, experience and training. For me, the best reason to learn them was to avoid the alternative – that poor recruit spent the next week on guard duty as a punishment!

There aren't many tales of bad discipline, poor hygiene or bad routine within the SAS for one simple reason: people don't make it through selection if they show those bad habits. When Colonel David Stirling formed the SAS, he had a simple ethos by which he and his men lived and worked: self-discipline, the unrelenting pursuit of excellence, humility and humour. These are good tenets for anyone to live by, but especially for Scouts and those living wild.

It doesn't matter if you're a Scout or a soldier, good personal admin is important. No one wants to be sharing with the guy who comes into the tent and deposits the contents of his rucksack on the floor. A good Scout has his kit packed at all times. If I put my hand into my pack, I know exactly where my torch is. Why? Because every good soldier knows the military motto, 'a place for everything, and everything in its place'. That way, you're always ready to go and you can be sure that some vital piece of equipment doesn't get left behind if you have to 'bug out' from your position. And as a Scout, you won't wake the whole tent if you need to nip to the loo at one o'clock in the morning and can't find your torch or your shoes!

A good Scout should always be asking if there is something that needs doing. Is there enough wood for this evening's campfire? Does the cook need a hand peeling spuds? Are all the pots and pans clean from dinner? Ask what needs to be done – don't wait to *be* asked. That way, no one will dine out on campfire stories about *you*, and you'll find yourself being invited back having made a name for yourself as a team player, someone with whom the other guys will want to share a tent and an adventure.

Chapter 7

BECOMING A PATHFINDER

the secrets of navigating safely and efficiently through all terrains in all weathers

Pathfinding is a skill that sets Scouts apart from almost everyone else. To be able to navigate yourself and your companions efficiently, confidently and accurately through all terrains in all weathers can literally be a lifesaving skill. And it's not just a skill for the Arctic or the Amazon. When you're living in the field, you are always susceptible to the elements, and being able to navigate effectively can mean the difference between the success of an expedition and its failure.

Anyone who is going out into the field should do what they can to hone their own pathfinding techniques rather than relying on the skills of others. The chances are that you'll be going into unfamiliar terrain and when that happens, every person is a potential unit of one. Groups get separated, injuries occur. What if you're the only person fit enough to go and find help? As a Scout it could be down to you, and you alone, to navigate everyone away from danger.

COMPASS AND MAP WORK

The compass is one of the oldest navigational tools known to man. People have been using them for hundreds of years – even before they even knew *why* they worked, realizing only that they *did* work.

How compasses work

It's very easy to make your own version of one of those early compasses, and it will teach you a lot. All you need are some needles, some wine-bottle corks, a bar magnet and a bowl of water. Using one end of the bar magnet, stroke a needle in the same direction several times. This will magnetize the needle. Stick the needle lengthways through the centre of a cork and then float the cork in the bowl of water. Do this with several needles and corks and you'll find that they all point in the same direction: north to south.

Anyone who has played around with magnets knows that the opposite ends – or poles – attract, while the same polarities repel each other. The compass made from a needle in water is doing exactly the same thing. The earth has its own magnetic field. One end of the magnetized needle is being attracted towards one end of the Earth's magnetic polarity – what we call magnetic north – while the other is being repelled.

Bearings

A bearing is the direction of a point in relation to north. If we used the points

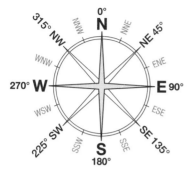

of a compass to describe where something is, we'd be rather limited – vaguely saying that something is to the north-east could actually mean that it's anywhere between north and east. This is not very helpful. Instead, we divide the directions into 360 degrees, with north at 0 degrees, as shown.

In this way, saying that our direction lies at, for example, 13° or 228° from our current position gives us a much more accurate way of describing which way we need to travel.

The two norths and magnetic variation

There is a problem with using magnetic north as a reference point for navigation: it changes. Drastically. Geologists have discovered that the Earth's magnetic field has in fact reversed its polarity several times during the planet's history and nobody really knows why. We also know that magnetic north drifts. It's currently somewhere over northern Canada. It is important to remember therefore that magnetic north is not a precise position, but rather a general area where the lines of the earth's magnetic force converge.

If our maps are going to be of any use whatsoever, they need to be drawn in relation to a fixed point, not a general area that moves anyway. The fixed point that cartographers use is the North Pole. In navigational terms, this is referred to as true north.

So here's the problem: north on your map is not the same as north on your compass. To add to our difficulties, here's a confusing scenario to consider. Imagine you're standing with a compass in a field in England, facing true north. Your compass, pointing to magnetic north, will be going off at an angle. Now imagine that you're standing between the North Pole and magnetic north, facing towards true north. Your compass will be pointing behind you, at a completely different angle to how it was in England. From this, we learn that the difference between magnetic north and true north *changes according to where you are on the Earth's surface.*

This difference between true north and magnetic north is called magnetic variation and it changes with time. If you're going to use a compass accurately, you need to know the magnetic variation of your position. A good map should tell you.

As I write this, I'm looking at an Ordnance Survey map, which states, 'Magnetic north is estimated at 3°35' west of grid north for July 2006. Annual change is approximately 09' east'. (Grid north is a third kind of north, but in the UK it is so close to true north that it makes little difference.) This tells me everything I need to know to use the map and compass together. If your map does not tell you the magnetic variation of your position you can look it up on the following website: www.ngdc.noaa.gov/geomagmodels/Declination.jsp

All you need now is the latitude and longitude of your position. It goes without saying that you should be doing these calculations before you set off on your trip.

In the pages that follow, you will need to adjust for magnetic variation. Sometimes this involves adding the magnetic variation; other times it involves subtracting it. You might want to remember this rhyme, which is taught to the armed forces so they can easily remember whether to add or subtract the magnetic variation:

Grid to mag[netic]: add | Mag[netic] to grid: get rid

This works when you have magnetic variation to the west. If the variation is to the east, the sums get reversed.

Types of compass

There are a number of different types of compass. For our purposes, the best is a Silva type.

This kind of compass has a needle set in liquid that stops it from flickering too much, a fixed baseplate and a dial with bearing degrees marked round it that can be rotated so that you can set a bearing and allow for magnetic variation.

Compass housing with degree dial

How to use a map and compass together

There are six basic skills you need to master when learning to use a map and compass together. To start with, they may seem complicated, but with practice they'll become second nature.

HIDDEN DANGERS

It's very important that you learn to understand and use magnetic variation. It might sound small, but for every 3° of variation that you forget to add on, you'll be 50 metres off course for each kilometre you travel. When you're trying to get to shelter or safety, the consequences of this can be very severe indeed.

The needle of a compass will always point to the strongest magnetic source it can detect. Nine times out of ten this will be the Earth's magnetic field but, sometimes, local magnetic sources can skew the reading. These magnetic sources can be man-made (watches, underground pipes and railway lines can all have magnetic fields); or they can be natural (some rocks, for example, can be magnetic if they contain metallic ores). Take readings regularly, and if you suspect that something is affecting your reading, move position slightly and take a new one.

IMPROVISING IN THE FIELD

You can make an improvised compass using a sewing needle. Magnetize the needle by rubbing it against your hair several times, making sure you rub it in the same direction each time. Lay the needle on a leaf or a piece of paper, and float it on a puddle or a bowl of water. It should align itself in a north-south direction.

To tell which is north and which is south, observe the position of the sun: before midday it will be in the east; after midday it will be in the west. Remember that the magnetic charge of the needle will only last for a short time – you'll need to recharge it by rubbing it on your hair again if you want to repeat the process.

TRAINING EXERCISES

It's crucial that you know how to use your compass and map before setting out into the field. Stuck in the middle of nowhere with the mist coming down and rain forecast is not a good time to start learning. Put your hands on a Silva type compass and an Ordnance Survey map of where you live and start training. It doesn't even matter if you live in the middle of a city: the principles are still the same, and learning how to navigate around fixed obstacles (like city centres!) is a very valuable exercise.

Following a bearing

This is an essential navigation technique. If you can see your destination, you can use your compass to work out which bearing it is on. Then, as you're walking towards it, you can constantly check that you're walking in the correct direction, even if you lose sight of your destination. When you're out in the field, it's surprising how often this happens: you might lose daylight, mist or rain could obscure your vision, or the lie of the land could change and obscure your view. To follow a bearing, follow these steps.

1. Hold the compass so that the direction of travel arrow points at your destination.

2. Turn the compass dial so that the orienting arrow is in line with the magnetic needle. *Remember to use the north end of the needle (which is usually red) and not the south end, otherwise you'll end up going 180 degrees in the wrong direction.*

3. The direction of travel arrow should now be in line with your bearing. Don't worry about adjusting for magnetic difference as you are plotting your destination in relation to where you are currently standing, and not in relation to a map.

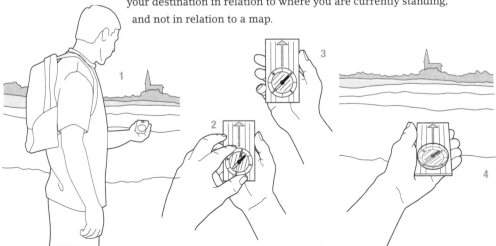

TRAINING EXERCISES

You can practise taking and following a bearing with a friend. Agree on a starting point, then one of you decide on a bearing, say 47°. Walk along that bearing for an agreed number of paces, then drop a coin on the floor. Tell your friend the bearing you followed and the number of paces you took, and see if they can locate the hidden treasure. If they manage it, the coin is theirs!

4. Now, as long as you keep your compass dial in the same position, whenever you line up your orienting arrow with the needle, your direction of travel arrow will point to your destination along the bearing you want to follow.

Setting a map

If you're using a map in unfamiliar territory, you need to ensure that your map is 'set' – pointing in the right direction. To do this, you need to know the magnetic variation for the area. A good map should indicate this; if it doesn't, make sure you know what it is before you set out.

1. Turn the compass dial so that the magnetic variation is shown against the index line. So, if the magnetic variation for the area is 3° west, that figure should be aligned with the pointer. Mag to grid, get rid: the dial should be set so that a bearing of 357° is shown against the index pointer.

2. Place the compass on the map with the direction of travel arrow parallel to the vertical grid lines and pointing towards the top of the map.

3. Keeping both the map and compass in this position, turn them both so the orienting arrow and needle line up.

4. Your map is now set and you should be able to identify features from the map all around you.

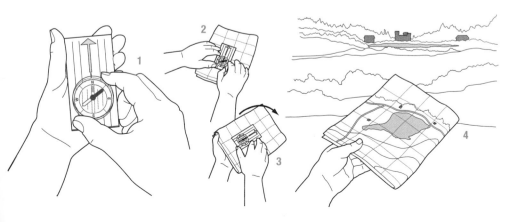

HIDDEN DANGERS

When you know the bearing you need to follow, write it down. Tired feet and a weary brain aren't conducive to good memory skills!

BEAR'S SECRET SCOUTING TIPS

When you're following a bearing, check it regularly – it's very easy to stray off course. Each time you check it, locate a landmark along that bearing, walk to the landmark then check the bearing again.

Setting a compass

If you have a map and can pinpoint where you are and where you want to go, this is how to set your compass so that it will keep pointing you in the correct direction.

1. Place the compass on your map and, using the long edge, join your starting point and finishing point together.

2. Turn the compass dial so that the orienting lines are parallel with the vertical grid lines on the map.

3. Take the compass from the map and use the compass dial to add the magnetic variation for your area (grid to mag, add). So, if your original bearing was 58° and your local magnetic variation is 3° west, set your compass so that the index line reads 61°.

4. Now turn the whole compass so that the needle and the orienting arrow line up. Your direction of travel arrow will be pointing the way you need to walk. Remember to keep checking your bearing at short, regular intervals.

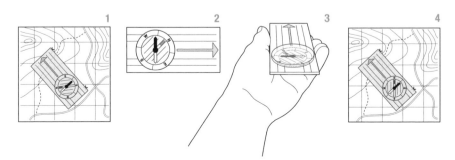

Plotting on a map the exact position of a landmark you can see

The technical name for this is intersection. It is a tried and tested army technique for locating enemy positions, targets and danger areas.

1. Locate at least two positions that you can identify on a map. You need to be able to see the object you are trying to plot from both these positions.

2. At the first position, take a bearing towards the object. Adjust for magnetic variation (mag to grid, get rid). Use your compass to draw a line on this bearing from your position.

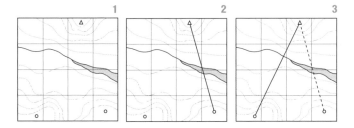

3. Move to the second position and repeat the process The two lines will intersect at the location of your object.

4. If you can do this from a third position, your intersection will be more accurate because you will have 'triangulated' it.

Back bearings

Getting to your destination is often only half the job. Sometimes you need to get back again. If you've been plotting your route by taking bearings, it's useful to know that you can reverse the process by using back bearings. Having travelled 200 paces from A to B at a bearing of 60°, you can return from B to A by travelling 200 paces at a bearing of 240°.

To work out a back bearing, you need to perform the following calculation:

If your original bearing was less than 180°, add 180° to calculate the back bearing.

If your original bearing was more than 180°, subtract 180° to calculate the back bearing.

Don't worry if you forget this formula. You'll know if you've done it wrong because you'll end up with a back bearing of less than 0° or more than 360°, which doesn't make sense.

Plotting your exact position on a map

The technical name for this is resection. If you're in the field with a map and compass and you know your general area but not your exact position, it's possible to plot exactly where you are using back bearings.

1. Locate two geographical features or landmarks that you can identify both in real life and on your map. If possible, make them about 90° apart relative to your position. (It's only possible to be approximate about this, of course, because you don't quite know your position!)

2. Take a bearing towards one of the landmarks. Adjust for magnetic variation (mag to grid, get rid).

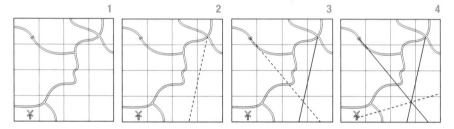

3. Now that you know the true bearing, you need to calculate the back bearing. On your map, use your compass to draw a line from the landmark on a back bearing towards your general area.

4. Do the same thing for the second landmark. The two lines should intersect at your exact position. If you can triangulate by using three landmarks, you'll get a more accurate reading.

Obstacles

In theory, you should be able to navigate directly to your destination using a map and compass. In practice, unfamiliar terrain is less obliging than that. It's more than likely that when you're following a bearing, you'll come across some obstacle – a ditch, perhaps, or a cliff face – that you have to navigate around. It may be that you can do this by sight; but often you can't, so you need to learn this technique.

Face your bearing. Now turn 90° in whichever direction appears most convenient. Walk in that direction; counting the number of paces you take. Once the obstacle is passed, turn 90° so that you are parallel to your original bearing. Walk forwards and, when you can, perform another

90° turn so that you are walking back to the line of your original bearing. Count the original number of paces. Perform one more 90° turn and you should be back on course.

READING MAPS

In the UK, we are lucky to have a source of extremely high-quality maps made by the Ordnance Survey. Not all maps are this good, so you need to make sure you can get the most out of them. To do this, you need to follow a few simple guidelines.

Most maps will have a legend, or key. You should study it closely. A good map will contain a huge quantity of very detailed information, but if you don't know what all the symbols mean you can never use them to their full advantage.

Once you have read and understood the legend, you need to check the age of the map so that you can work out the current magnetic variation.

Finally, you need to establish the scale of your map, and make clear in your head the meaning of all the contour lines.

Scale

Scale is a ratio of size. The larger the scale of your map, the more detailed it will be. The scale of the map you choose depends on what you're using it for. For example, a detailed, large-scale map would be totally useless to a fighter pilot who would zoom across the area it shows in seconds. By the same token, a soldier on the ground would find a small-scale aeronautical map just as useless because it would not give the level of detail he needs.

All maps will clearly tell you what their scale is, and for pathfinding purposes a map scale of 1:50,000 is suitable; 1:25,000 is fantastic (the smaller the numbers in the ratio, the more detailed the map).

A scale of 1:50,000 means every one unit on the map is equivalent to 50,000 units in real life. Another way of thinking of it is 2cm to 1km – 2cm on the map is equivalent to 1km in real life. Or simpler still, 1 box is 1km (this also applies for 1:25,000 maps). Once you know the scale of your map, you can judge distances more easily.

Some compasses have scale rules along the side of the base plate, which convert distances from common scales into real-life distances. This saves you having to do the calculation for yourself.

| Contour lines

Maps are flat. The surface of the earth isn't. How, then, does a map describe altitude?

Contour lines are lines on a map that join areas of equivalent height. On a 1:50,000 map they are normally drawn at 10-metre intervals; on a 1:25,000 map they are normally drawn at 5-metre intervals. On a good map, some of the contour lines will give elevation figures (see example below).

You'll soon get used to interpreting contour lines at a glance. The rule of thumb is that lots of them close together indicate a sharp incline; if they're more spaced out, the incline is gentle; and if there are none, the terrain is flat. As you get more experienced with maps, you will start to recognize certain geographical features according to the shape of the contour lines.

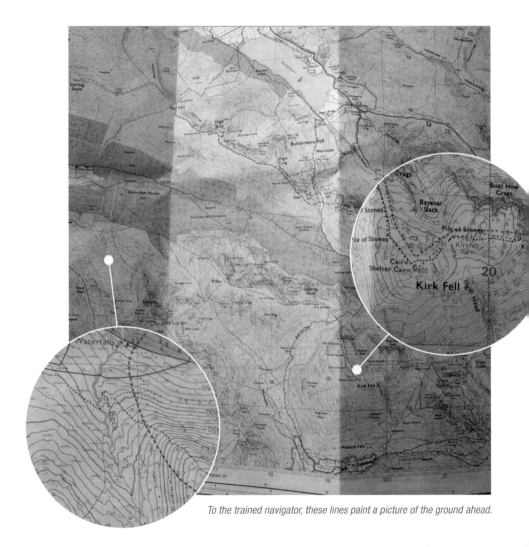

To the trained navigator, these lines paint a picture of the ground ahead.

ROUTE SELECTION

More often than not, you'll have a specific route in mind with a fixed starting point and destination. If this is the case, it's important that you study the map well before you leave. Even if you're part of a group where the responsibility for navigating lies with somebody else, you should spend time with a map beforehand and understand the route that you're going to take.

Embarking on a trek with no idea of the route you're going to take is a bad idea. Preparation is key. When you're planning a route, there are several things you should take into consideration.

- Access routes. If you're being taken in country by vehicle, check your map carefully to ensure that the access routes are suitable. Many aren't, and if you can't get to your starting point, your expedition is over before it's even begun.

- Campsites. If you're staying out for one or more nights, where are you going to pitch camp? Think about access to water, fuel and shelter. Is the ground exposed or open? Will you need to take a tent, or are you going to be in terrain that will provide what you need for man-made shelters?

- What is the topography of your route? Does it take you up steep inclines that will tire you out more quickly and so reduce the amount of ground you can cover in a day?

- Does your route take you across water? If so, how will you cross it? Will you have to walk miles out of your way to find a bridge? Is the ground likely to be well drained and dry, or marshy and difficult to walk through? (On SAS selection, we learned to dread the little symbols on a map that indicated 'marshy ground'. This was often the biggest understatement ever, as we waded through knee-deep gloop for hour after hour!)

- Does your route take you above the treeline? This is the height above which trees do not grow, usually because of colder temperatures. Expeditions that go above the treeline require particular skills, clothing and equipment – mountain tents because of winds, cold-weather clothing, crampons if it's icy, and extra fuel as there's no wood to burn.

- Are there enough geographical features and landmarks for you to take bearings from, and to navigate with precision?

- What are the prevailing weather conditions? How will they affect the geography of your route?

Unless you're setting out specifically to challenge yourself, you should always choose the route that offers the least resistance in terms of geography. Gentle slopes, established paths and natural waterways will all make your expedition potentially less perilous.

TIME AND DISTANCE

How far you've travelled, and how far you've yet to go, are important things to know. In these days of road signs and speedometers, they are also things we are used to knowing when we're out in the car for the day. So surely it's the same in the field, right?

Unfortunately not – measuring distance by foot on varied, undulating terrain is notoriously difficult. Maps will give you an idea of distance as the crow flies, but this will not take into account hills, valleys and other obstacles. An approximation is the best you're likely to get. Having said that, there are situations when approximations of distance and time are not only useful, they're essential.

I remember once on SAS selection searching out a small checkpoint tent on the top of a very exposed, boggy plateau during a windy, snowy winter's night. I had been walking for 17 hours and I was cold, wet and hungry. It was the last checkpoint I needed to locate before heading off the mountains back to the trucks. Visibility was down to almost nothing as I huddled in a peat crater to study the map. My objective was only 250 metres away, but I knew that if I got it wrong I could be up there for hours, staggering around in vain in such low visibility. I took longer than usual to calculate an accurate bearing, along with magnetic variation and pacing. I counted the steps religiously and at the end of the pacing I slipped down a boggy bank and actually landed on top of the tent I had been aiming for. I thought, good job, Bear! The directing staff inside the tent, however, were less than impressed when a size-11 boot ripped through the flap!

There are various methods that we use to measure and approximate distance and time in the field.

Naismith's Rule

Naismith's Rule is a rule of thumb that will give you a rough idea of how long a route, or section of a route, is likely to take. It was worked out by William Naismith, a Scottish mountaineer, at the end of the nineteenth century and is still used today.

Naismith's Rule states that you should allow one hour for every 5 kilometres going forward, and add an extra half an hour for every 300 metres of ascent. So, a hike of 15 kilometres with an ascent of 500 metres should take about 4 hours.

There are, of course, all sorts of variables that will affect this – your general fitness levels, the weight of your pack, the ruggedness of the terrain and weather conditions are always big factors. Lots of people have tried to make Naismith's Rule more accurate with all sorts of complicated charts and tables, but the truth is that everyone's a bit different. The more you hike, the better you will become at judging how long it will take you to cross different types of terrain: Naismith's Rule can serve as a starting point for your own personal formula, so test it and adjust it to fit your stride and level of fitness. You should also remember that groups tend to travel less quickly than individuals because they can only go as fast as their slowest member.

Using our eyes to judge distance

When we look at an object in the distance, the line of sight from each of our eyes converges.

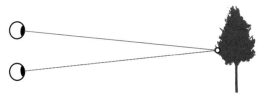

Our brains learn that when our eyes are converged at a particular angle, that angle is associated with a certain distance. (If you've ever watched a baby trying to grab a toy, you'll see that at first they'll be clumsy and unable to do it. That's because his or her brain has not yet learned the distances associated with the convergence of their lines of sight.)

There are various environmental factors, however, that encourage our brains to play tricks on us. These can make distances appear closer or further away than they actually are. If you want to judge distances effectively in the field, you need to be aware of the following factors.

Things appear closer than they are when:

- it's a very bright day
- the sun is shining behind you
- you are lower down than the object you're observing
- the object is bigger than other things around it
- there is dead ground between you and the object

Things appear further away than they are when:

- lighting conditions are poor
- the sun is shining towards you
- the object is smaller than other things around it
- you're lying down
- you're looking across a valley or down a street

Bracketing

Bracketing is a military technique that is used to pinpoint distance. When artillery shells are fired at an enemy position, the distance between the artillery and the target is often unknown, or at least only known approximately. In instances such as this, the artillery will fire beyond the target, then short of the target. These two parameters will give them an idea of where they should finally aim.

The same technique can be used for non-military purposes. While it might not be possible to judge a distance precisely, it is often possible to estimate that the point you are aiming for is, for example, no less than 800 metres and no more than 1 kilometre away. Then, if you walk for more than about a kilometre without reaching your intended point, you know you've gone wrong.

Another bracketing technique is to use your 'no less than' and 'no more than' figures to estimate an actual distance. So, if something is no closer than 800 metres and no further than 1 kilometre, you can take the average of these two figures and say that your object is about 900 metres away.

Similarly, if you are plotting a course, it's a great help if you can think of your path as travelling between landmarks, rather than insisting on strict point-to-point navigation. A path lined with prominent features is quicker and easier to follow than a pre-set straight line.

Bracketing is an incredibly useful technique because it takes away the need for precision, which is something you can rarely achieve in the field.

Units of measure

If you're like most people, you probably find it difficult to estimate distances in terms of metres. Even if you do feel confident enough to describe a landmark as being, say, 200 metres away, there's no guarantee that the person you're describing that to will be able to judge exactly what it means. User measures are another military way of getting round this problem by describing distances in terms of common objects – football pitches or swimming pools, for example. For many people 'two football pitches' is a more meaningful approximation than 'about 200 metres'.

Remember, when you're approximating distances in the field, there's no prize for mathematical accuracy. It's far better to describe things in a way people can easily understand.

Appearance method

A third army technique for judging distance is the appearance method, where the amount of detail you can see on a person tells you roughly how far away from you that person is.

At 100m the person can be seen clearly

At 200m the colour of their skin is just identifiable, all other details clear

At 300m the body outline is clear, most other details are blurred

At 400m the body outline is clear, all other details blurred

At 500m the body appears tapered, the head is indistinct

At 600m the body is wedge-shaped, the head cannot be seen

At 100m   *At 200m*

At 300m

At 400m

These distances will, of course, change according to a person's eyesight and how clear the view is.

| Pacing techniques

If you know the average length of your pace, you can use it to approximate distances. To work out your pace, take 100 paces along a distance you know you can calibrate, like a sports track. Divide that distance by 100 to give you the average length of one pace. Do this several times and take the average of your results. You will then know roughly how far you walk with each step.

My preferred method is to walk, say, 100 metres and count the number of paces you take. Repeat this several times and take the average of the number of paces. You now know roughly how many paces you take to cover 100 metres.

Of course, there are plenty of problems with this technique. When you're in the field, your pace length is determined by the territory: you'll take smaller steps up a rocky slope than you will over a flat field. But it's worth knowing your pace length. You never know when it will get you out of trouble.

BEAR'S SECRET SCOUTING TIPS

Keeping track of the number of paces you've taken can be a real problem, especially if you're measuring reasonably long distances – the smallest distraction will make you forget your pace count. You can use a pedometer, a mechanical device that swings a pendulum every time you take a step, and then keeps count. However, these are very unreliable in the field. An army technique is to use a pacer – you've probably seen them being used when air stewards count the number of people on a plane. With every ten paces, you make one click on the pacer, which records the number of clicks you've made – ten clicks means 100 paces. Or you could fill one pocket with small stones. Each time you reach 100 paces, move one stone to your other pocket. That way you've got a fixed reminder of how far you've come. Alternatively, use a line of beads on a string like an abacus.

Bear Drinks Tea For Breakfast

My final tip when it comes to navigating using a map and compass is this: you need to rely on a combination of many different factors to give you accurate information. Don't just rely on your bearing. The main factors you should rely upon are bearing, distance, time, features and backdrop. I have a mnemonic to remember this: **B**ear **D**rinks **T**ea **F**or **B**reakfast.

Bearing – what bearing should I be following?
Distance – how far is my next destination?
Time – how long, using Naismith's Rule, should I take to reach my next destination?
Features – what prominent features or landmarks should I see en route (such as a canal on my left or a wood on my right)?
Backdrop – what will I reach or see that will tell me I have overshot my destination? (For example, if I'm starting to go downhill, I must have come too far.)

These are the main principles that I use to navigate, and they have saved my skin many a time!

GLOBAL POSITIONING SYSTEMS (GPS)

GPS was initially developed for military purposes by the United States Department for Defense, and GPS products are an essential part of a Special Forces soldier's kit. Nowadays, of course, they're commonplace – people have them in their cars and even on their phones. These clever little machines use satellites circling the earth. The unit requires a clear 'sight' of at least three of these satellites in order to triangulate the user's position. GPS is getting better on an almost daily basis. There are now even 'deep probe' GPS units, designed to work even through a thick canopy in the jungle – a potential lifesaver for troops on ops in such terrain.

GPS can be incredibly useful. If you have a GPS device, and it doesn't take up too much room in your pack, by all means take it. However – and I can't stress this enough – you should never rely on GPS to the detriment of your basic navigational skills. Too many things can go wrong with them: if your GPS device goes down and you don't know how to navigate out of unfamiliar territory, you're in trouble. This is a good example of technology being a great bonus, but a lousy replacement for well-honed fieldcraft skills.

NAVIGATING BY THE STARS

Navigating by the stars – astronavigation – is one of the oldest navigation methods known to man. It's easy to see why. The stars were there before maps and compasses, and a *long* time before GPS! Astronavigation was traditionally used by sailors who, in the absence of fixed markers in the middle of the ocean from which to take bearings, would use the moon and a total of 57 navigational stars to find their way.

If you look up into the sky on a clear night in the countryside where there is no ambient light to spoil your view, the number and clarity of the stars can be breathtaking – in my opinion it's one of the highlights of being in the wilderness. It can also be a bit daunting: with so many stars up there, how will you ever learn which ones will lead you in the right direction? And don't they move anyway?

Astronavigation can certainly be a very in-depth study. But a small amount of knowledge can be a big help if you're navigating at night because you can use the stars to determine direction. Which stars you use depends on which hemisphere you're in.

The northern hemisphere

In the northern hemisphere, the most useful star is the North Star (Polaris). If you walk towards this star, you will always be heading north; and from that you can work out the other directions.

Contrary to popular myth, the North Star *isn't* the brightest star in the sky. It is,

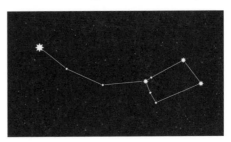

however, easy to locate if you learn to recognize three constellations: Ursa Minor (the Little Dipper), Ursa Major (the Big Dipper or the Plough) and Cassiopeia.

The North Star is the final star in the handle of the saucepan shape of Ursa Minor (right).

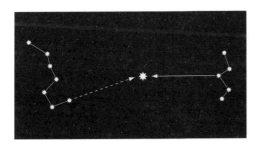

However, it is not always possible to see Ursa Minor. If this is the case, you need to look for Ursa Major and Cassiopeia (left).

If you draw a straight line from the two stars at the end of Ursa Major's 'bowl', you will come to Polaris. It is about four times the length between the last two stars of Ursa Major along the same line of direction. Cassiopeia looks like a wonky W or M on its side. If you follow a line straight out from the centre star of Cassiopeia, you'll reach Polaris. It's about halfway between the two constellations.

BEAR'S SECRET SCOUTING TIPS

If you're at the North Pole, Polaris will be directly above you. And because the earth's axis is constantly changing, so the star directly above the North Pole changes. This means that Polaris has not always been the North Star, nor will it always be. In time, the star Gamma Cephei will become closer to the pole than Polaris and so will become the North Star. You don't need to worry about that too much, however – it won't happen for another thousand years!

The southern hemisphere

Polaris can't be seen from most of the southern hemisphere, so there you need to use a different constellation, the Southern Cross. This will help you

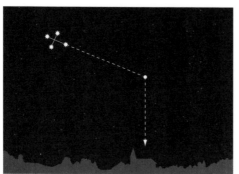

work out which way is south.

Imagine extending the long axis of the Southern Cross to five times its length. From this imaginary point in the sky, follow a vertical line down towards the earth. The direction from where you are to that point on the ground will be south.

What if it's cloudy?

Astronavigation depends – obviously – on being able to see the stars. If the sky is totally clouded over, there's not much you can do. If, however, there is only partial cloud, you can still work out if a particular star is in the north, south, east or west by observing its movement through the sky. Take two sticks, the rear stick needs to be shorter than the front one; place them in the ground one behind the other and about 60cm apart. Line the two tips up with your star so that you are looking at all three at once along the same line. Continue observing. After a while, the star will have moved in relation to the two static tips.

In the northern hemisphere:

- ✦ movement to the left means the star is in the north
- ✦ movement to the right means the star is in the south
- ✦ movement upwards means the star is in the east
- ✦ movement downwards means the star is in the west

In the southern hemisphere, this is reversed:

- ✦ movement to the left means the star is in the south
- ✦ movement to the right means the star is in the north
- ✦ movement upwards means the star is in the west
- ✦ movement downwards means the star is in the east

If the star doesn't move at all, you've lucked out: that's the North Star!

NAVIGATING BY THE SUN

Solar navigation, like astronavigation, is a time-honoured method of finding your way. There are two methods of doing this: the staff method and the watch method.

The staff method

This method works in northern temperate zones (from the Tropic of Cancer to the Arctic Circle) and southern temperate zones (from the Tropic of Capricorn to the Antarctic Circle).

Find a straight stick about a metre long and stick it in the ground where it will cast a definite shadow. Mark the point where the tip of the shadow falls (1). Wait for about 15 minutes. The shadow will move. Mark the tip of the second shadow. Draw a line from the first mark to the second mark and about 30cm beyond (2). Stand with your left foot on the first point and your right foot on the second (3).

If you are in a northern temperate zone, you are now facing approximately north; in a southern temperate zone you are facing approximately south.

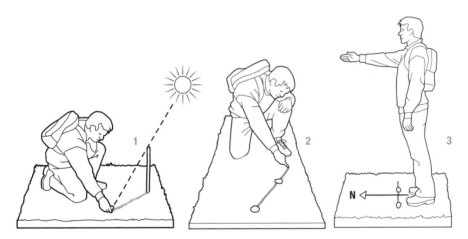

The watch method

This is a handy method of getting a rough direction, but it's not as accurate as the staff method. The closer you are to the equator, the less accurate it is.

To orientate yourself using your watch, you need to make sure it is telling the accurate local time. If a daylight-saving hour has been added, you need to wind the watch back an hour.

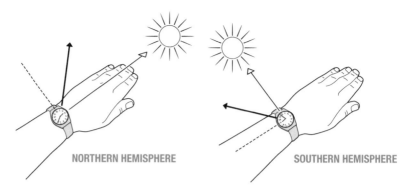

NORTHERN HEMISPHERE   SOUTHERN HEMISPHERE

If you're in the northern hemisphere, lay your watch flat with the hour hand pointing towards the sun. A good way of doing this is by laying it on a flat surface, then putting your eye at the same level of the watch. Now, draw an imaginary line from the centre of the watch that bisects the angle between the hour hand and the figure 12 on the dial. This direction is south.

In the southern hemisphere, you need to point the figure 12 on your watch towards the sun, then bisect the angle between the hour hand and 12 o'clock. This direction is north.

WEATHER LORE

First, a caveat: predicting the weather is a complicated business. Professional weather forecasters have all manner of complicated equipment and computer modelling systems, and sometimes (in fact, quite often) even they get it wrong.

Having said that, nature can give you some pretty hefty clues about what the weather's about to do. You just need to learn how to interpret these clues. It's an essential skill in the field: getting caught in bad weather can be more than inconvenient. It can be life threatening.

I was caught out recently in a lightning storm in one of the most volatile weather places in the USA – the Black Hills of Dakota. The thunder and lightning and lashing rain were so ferocious that it was impossible to hold a conversation, even shouting. Only 30 minutes earlier there had been a gentle breeze and sunshine. Like an idiot, I had been having a nap! Hey, we can't always get it right...

| Clouds

It doesn't take a great deal of insider information to recognize a big heavy storm cloud. We've all seen them. If you know a bit more about other clouds and their behaviour, however, you're going to be a lot better at predicting the weather.

When looking at a cloud, there are two things you need to determine: its height and its shape. There are three levels of cloud:

- High-level clouds (above about 6,000 metres) have names that include the word cirro or cirrus.

- Medium-level clouds (between 2,000 and 6,000 metres) have names starting with the word alto.

- Low-level clouds (below 2,000 metres) have all sorts of different names.

There are three principle cloud shapes:

- Cirriform are feathery clouds.
- Stratiform are sheets of cloud.
- Cumuliform are heaps of cloud.

Clouds tend to behave as they look – if they look bad or benign, they probably are!

If you can tell the height and type of cloud, you can predict with a certain degree of accuracy what type of weather you can expect.

	Cloud type	Description	Likely weather
High clouds	Cirrus	Thin, wispy streaks/ 'mare's tails'	Fine weather, then rain (NB Cirrus are difficult to interpret. Some denser types of cirrus denote no change)
	Cirrocumulus	'Mackerel sky'/ 'rippled sand'	Showers
	Cirrostratus	Amorphous cloud/ halo effects	Rain
Medium clouds	Altocumulus	Dimpled heap cloud	Showers
	Altostratus	Watery sun	Rain
Low clouds	Stratocumulus	Heaped layer cloud	No change
	Stratus	Amorphous layer cloud	Drizzle
	Nimbostratus	Layered cloud stacked high	Storm
	Cumulus	Heaped fluffy cloud	Good weather
	Cumulonimbus	Fluffy cloud heaped very high	Thunderstorm

| Wind

Wind can be unpredictable and difficult to interpret. Different areas have their different prevailing winds and they are affected by the arrival of warm and cold fronts. In temperate regions, however, there is a rule of thumb called the crosswinds rule. Stand with your back to the wind and look for medium-level or high-level clouds. If, in the northern hemisphere, they are moving from left to right, you can expect bad weather; if they're moving from right to left, you can expect the weather to improve. In the southern hemisphere, reverse these directions.

Interpreting wind speeds

Ships on the open sea are particularly susceptible to strong winds, but historically there was a problem with describing these winds: one man's gentle breeze could be another man's strong breeze. In the nineteenth century a British admiral called Sir Francis Beaufort set about trying to standardize the way people describe wind speeds. The Beaufort Scale is still in use today.

Beaufort number	Description of the wind	Speed of the wind in knots	Possible effects of the wind
0	Calm	<1	Smoke rises vertically
1	Light air	1–3	Direction of the wind is shown by smoke drifting but not by a weather vane
2	Light breeze	4–6	Wind felt on the face; leaves rustle; weather vanes move in the wind
3	Gentle breeze	7–10	Leaves and twigs in constant motion; the wind extends a light flag
4	Moderate breeze	11–16	Dust and loose paper are raised; the small branches of trees are moved
5	Fresh breeze	17–21	Small trees begin to sway; small crested waves form on inland waters
6	Strong breeze	22–27	Large branches of trees begin to move; telegraph wires whistle; umbrellas are difficult to use
7	Moderate gale	28–33	Whole trees are set in motion; some difficulty in walking against the wind; swaying of skyscrapers may be felt by those on the upper floors
8	Fresh gale	34–40	Twigs break off trees; great difficulty in walking against the wind
9	Strong gale	41–47	Slight structural damage to buildings; chimney pots and slates removed
10	Whole gale	48–55	Trees are uprooted; extensive damage to buildings
11	Storm	56–63	Widespread damage
12	Hurricane	>64	The whole countryside is devastated

Wind-chill factor

The wind can have a huge effect on how warm it actually feels. The wind-chill factor is the apparent temperature warm-blooded creatures feel during windy conditions. If you look at the table overleaf, you'll see the sort of effect it has. So, if you're planning an expedition and the forecast is for wind, don't ignore it: it can have a big effect on the route you take and how long your expedition is likely to last. I have learned that in cold, wet weather, it is rarely the cold or wet that kills you. It's the wind that does the damage. Cold and wet is one thing – add wind into the equation and you have a potentially lethal combination. Be aware of that and act accordingly – get protection from the wind as soon as you can.

Wind Chill Index

	Temperature (°C)																	
Calm	4	2	-1	-4	-7	-9	-12	-15	-18	-21	-23	-26	-29	-32	-34	-37	-40	-43
5	2	0	-4	-7	-10	-14	-17	-21	-24	-27	-30	-33	-37	-40	-43	-47	-49	-54
10	1	-3	-6	-9	-13	-16	-20	-23	-27	-30	-33	-37	-41	-44	-47	-51	-54	-58
15	0	-4	-7	-10	-14	-18	-22	-25	-28	-32	-36	-39	-42	-46	-50	-53	-57	-61
20	-1	-4	-8	-12	-16	-19	-23	-26	-30	-34	-37	-41	-44	-48	-52	-56	-59	-63
25	-2	-5	-9	-13	-16	-20	-24	-27	-31	-35	-38	-42	-46	-50	-53	-57	-61	-64
30	-2	-5	-9	-13	-17	-21	-24	-28	-32	-36	-39	-43	-47	-51	-55	-58	-62	-66
35	-2	-6	-10	-14	-18	-22	-25	-29	-33	-37	-41	-44	-48	-52	-56	-60	-63	-67
40	-3	-7	-10	-14	-18	-22	-26	-30	-34	-38	-42	-46	-49	-53	-57	-61	-64	-68
45	-3	-7	-11	-15	-19	-23	-27	-31	-34	-38	-42	-46	-50	-54	-58	-62	-65	-69
50	-3	-7	-11	-16	-19	-23	-27	-31	-35	-39	-42	-47	-51	-55	-59	-63	-67	-71
55	-4	-8	-12	-16	-19	-24	-28	-32	-36	-39	-43	-48	-52	-56	-59	-63	-67	-72
60	-4	-8	-12	-16	-20	-24	-28	-32	-36	-40	-44	-48	-52	-56	-60	-64	-68	-72

Wind (mph)

Frostbite times   30 minutes   10 minutes   5 minutes

Old wives' tales

It might seem a bit odd talking about these after the scientific precision of the Beaufort Scale and the wind-chill index. But most of these old sayings have some basis in fact; and they'll be a lot more use to you in the field where you often have to make speedy decisions based on brief observations of the conditions around you.

- *Red sky at night, shepherd's delight; red sky at morning, shepherd's warning.* A red sky at dusk is often due to the sun shining through dust particles that are suspended in a high-pressure system. High pressure often brings dry, warm air – in other words, a delight. If the red sky is seen in the morning, it means the high pressure is in the east where the sun rises and has moved past you, probably bringing a low-pressure system in its wake. Low pressure often brings moisture. (This theory works on the assumption that the prevailing northern hemisphere weather goes from west to east.) Don't confuse a red sky with a red sun.

- *When a halo rings the moon or sun, rain's approaching on the run.* These halos are caused by ice crystals in high cirrostratus clouds, and will very likely bring rain.

- *Mackerel skies and mare's tails, make tall ships take in their sails.*
  Cirrus clouds often precede wind or rain.

- *Rainbow to windward, foul fall the day; rainbow to leeward, rain runs away.*
  If the wind is heading towards you from a rainbow, it is often bringing the
  rain that caused the rainbow in your direction.

EMERGENCY SIGNALS

Most of us have mobile phones these days and could easily use them should
we need to alert people to the fact that we are in danger. It would be foolish
to underestimate their importance as an emergency signalling device. If you
have a mobile phone, you should take it with you.

However, much like GPS units, you shouldn't rely on your mobile. Batteries
run out and in much of the terrain you're likely to find yourself, network
coverage will probably be patchy. So, you need to know how to send up distress
signals using traditional methods that have stood the test of time.

Fire is the most effective means of signalling. A triangle is the international
distress signal, so in extreme survival situations people are recommended to
build three fires to attract the attention of overhead aircraft. However, if you're
on your own it is often too difficult to keep three fires going; and in any case, for
most purposes one big, blazing fire is more effective than three smaller ones.

When you're building a signal fire,
you need to make it burn as fast and
as hot as possible. This will give off the
maximum amount of light during the
hours of darkness, and a thick plume
of white smoke during the day – use
wet leaves or green wood for smoke.
(Smoke signals, of course, are only
effective on calm days: high winds,
rain or snow will disperse the smoke.)
If you can get your hands on spruce
trees or birch bark, you'll find that
these will burn extremely well. Just
make sure you're careful to keep the
fire under control.

*Fire and smoke are excellent means of
signalling in an emergency.*

The ability to read a map and use a compass is fundamental to scouting and soldiering. If you can't *get* somewhere, you can't *do* whatever it is you intended to do in the first place. But just being able to read and interpret a map and compass is only part of the story: you need to be able to read the ground, the weather and all the signs of nature as well.

Even before Baden-Powell formed the Scout movement, he recognized the importance of map-reading as one of the key skills all good Scouts and soldiers should have. He recalled the lead-up to the Boer War when, before hostilities broke out, he was sent out on a reconnaissance of the passes of the Drakensberg Mountains in South Africa. After a lot of map-to-ground study, Baden-Powell realized that there were a number of discrepancies in the maps they had. He reported this discovery, knowing that it was strategically of vital importance; but its value was not recognized at the time and when the Boer War did break out his corrections to the maps had not been recorded. To make matters worse his advice against holding the town of Ladysmith – based on his knowledge of the area – was ignored and the British suffered a disastrous defeat during the subsequent siege.

From that day on, Baden-Powell insisted that all his troops and, consequently, all Scouts, should have a thorough understanding of maps, compasses and map-reading. More importantly, they should be able to use that knowledge effectively.

The subject of map-reading, or at least the accuracy of an individual's map-reading, is the reason for many a joke between soldiers – if anyone's navigation is ever in doubt, they are not allowed to forget it in a hurry! I recall one incident when a patrol was on a training exercise in the desert. They were tasked to put in an OP (Observation Post) overlooking a small village. A local helicopter pilot was engaged to insert them. When briefed, he assured the patrol commander that he knew the bridge over a *wadi* – a dry riverbed – that was marked on the map. In reality, however, he dropped them off at a bridge that was 20 kilometres north of the intended drop-off point, because it looked the same and they were 'in the area'! As you can imagine, this particular pilot's navigation skills were not trusted again. Luckily, no real harm was done, other than the troops having a very tiring walk that lasted all night, but the patrol was glad of their navigation skills as they made their way to the correct drop-off point.

Such a mistake can sometimes be far more dangerous. All too frequently the emergency services are called out to rescue people on mountain and moor who have misinterpreted the map and got themselves hopelessly lost. A good Scout should never be the reason for such an incident. Learn how to navigate, practise as often as you can and you won't become an emergency-service statistic or, even worse, a casualty that has succumbed to the elements.

Anybody can achieve basic proficiency at map and compass work, and it can literally save lives. GPS makes our lives even easier, but never forget the basics. Finally, whenever you do go out with your friends to practise, always tell someone when and where you are going, your intended route and, very importantly, when you expect to return. Remember: always trust your compass not your instincts. The compass is always right – unless you are a soldier who has not made the route in time on SAS selection, in which case the excuse is always that the compass was wrong!

NATURE'S WATCH

identifying, tracking, stalking and close observation of wildlife

'Every animal is interesting to watch, and it is just as difficult to stalk a weasel as it is to stalk a lion.'

Lord Robert Baden-Powell, K.C.B.

We don't own the land that we trek through; we share it with hundreds of other creatures. You'd be forgiven for forgetting this, however, if you were unskilled in the art of observation. On a walk through the woods, it can often seem that there are no animals for miles around. This is almost never true. If you know what you're looking for, and how to find it, the natural world provides you with access to an amazing variety of wildlife. To come across these animals in their natural habitat is one of the greatest thrills of living wild. There's an overwhelming sense of achievement when you manage to track a wild animal to within metres, then stalk it close enough to be able to photograph it without it knowing you are there.

If you're going to experience this thrill, you need to be trained to observe and learn how to conceal yourself. These are two sides of the same coin. As army recruits are taught, to observe is to see through your enemy's concealment; to conceal is to avoid his observation. Scouts can use these skills as part of their formidable arsenal.

I once trained with the San Bushmen in Namibia, southern Africa – one of the best hunter–tracker tribes still around today. Watching how they move and observe as they cover ground was such a privilege. What was just a bush or a bit of scrub to the untrained eye was a wealth of information to the Bushmen. As they moved, they observed, quietly chatted and confirmed each sign they had seen; then they tracked, followed, listened (and often had a smoke!) before finally closing in, having tracked a hare back to its 'form'. Once there, they would dig the

The San Bushmen's tracking skills are incredible.

hare out and that would be their dinner – minimal effort, maximum brain – pitting their skills against the animals'. Such abilities take generations to hone, but there is much we can learn from tribes such as the San Bushmen that will enable us as Scouts to become highly efficient and tactical trackers ourselves.

OBSERVATION SKILLS

Before you can track anything, you have to know *how* to look; and before you can conceal yourself, you need to know how other creatures look at you. That might sound easy – after all, we're always looking at things, aren't we? In fact, there's looking and there's *looking*: true observation is a skill that can be learned and practised, and is something at which you can never stop improving.

Why things are seen

There are six main reasons why things are seen: shape, shadow, silhouette, surface, spacing and movement.

Shape

We learn to associate objects according to their outline or shape, especially if that shape contrasts with its surroundings. The human body is a very distinctive shape if it is not properly camouflaged.

Shadow

In sunlight, an object can cast a shadow even though it's out of sight itself, and as the sun moves, so does the shadow. An object that's already in shadow can't cast one.

Good camouflage is all about disguising the distinctive head and shoulder shape.

Silhouette

A silhouette is the outline of an object against a plain background, such as sky, water or a plain open field. If the background is changed to something uneven, it's less likely that a silhouette will be seen.

Surface

If an object's surface is different to its surroundings, it will be seen. Human skin, for example, is visible against most natural backgrounds, as are shiny objects.

If you're smart, nature can conceal you effectively.

Spacing

Look around you. Nothing in nature is evenly spaced. Only man-made objects show regular spacing.

Movement

We could stare and stare at an animal well camouflaged by its terrain and not know it's there. As soon as it moves, however, our eyes will quickly be alerted to its presence. When you're looking for creatures in the wild, you need to be very sensitive to movement; and be aware that your own movement will give you away.

Kim's Game

Scouts and soldiers alike employ an exercise called Kim's Game. It derives its name from Rudyard Kipling's novel *Kim* about an orphan brought up on the streets of India. He falls under the influence of a jewel merchant called Lurgan Sahib who is, in fact, a secret service operative. Over time, Lurgan Sahib trains Kim for secret service work. As part of this training, he encourages Kim to play a game with a young Hindu boy. He lays out fifteen jewels; the two players look at the jewels, then they are covered up. Kim and the Hindu boy have to describe as many of the stones as they can. The Hindu child wins.

'He is thy master,' said Lurgan Sahib, smiling.

'Huh! He knew the names of the stones,' said Kim, flushing. 'Try again! With common things such as he and I know.'

They heaped the tray again with odds and ends gathered from the shop, and even the kitchen, and every time the child won, until Kim marvelled.

'Bind my eyes – let me feel once with my fingers, and even *then* I will leave thee open-eyed behind,' he challenged.

Kim stamped with vexation when the lad made his boast good.

'If it were men, or horses,' he said, 'I could do better. This playing with tweezers and knives and scissors is too little.'

'Learn first – teach later,' said Lurgan Sahib. 'Is he thy master?'

'Truly. But how is it done?'

'By doing it many times over till it is done perfectly – for it is worth doing.'

Kim was being trained as a spy and this game was crucial to that training because it taught him the skill of observing and memorizing small things. In the military, the word Kim is used as an acronym – Keep In Memory – and Kim's Game is a brilliant starting point for training yourself to become a keen observer. Start with a small number of objects and build your way up. The more you do this, the better trained your mind will become. If you keep it up, you'll find that you start memorizing what you observe almost automatically. You'll become a natural detective and, in the business of observation, that's no bad thing.

How to look

Kim's Game is a great exercise for training your brain. In the field, however, observation is more difficult because the range of your vision is greatly increased and there's much more to see and process. If you're presented with an open space, there's no point in just gazing randomly at it because you'll see everything and nothing at the same time. Instead, you should learn a technique known as 'casting', which outdoorsmen have used for generations.

Imagine dropping a stone into a clear lake. You would see concentric rings rippling out from the point of impact. Now imagine you are standing at the point of impact. Your vision needs to follow the patterns you see in front of you. Scan the area ahead in a left-to-right semicircle, about 2 metres forward and 3 metres wide. Make sure you pick up any little detail of the ground ahead, and remember why things are seen: shape, shadow, silhouette, surface, spacing and movement. Be on the lookout for all these things.

Now move your eyes to another semicircle in front of the first and scan from right to left. Repeat this process until you've scanned about 15 metres ahead of you. As you go, look up as well as down, into the treetops; and make sure you examine the ground where you are standing – it's all too easy to be right on top of something you're looking for and not even notice it.

When we look at views from different perspectives, we notice things we hadn't seen before. So, you should occasionally turn around and look back the way you've come, just in case.

If you're trying to observe tracks in the ground,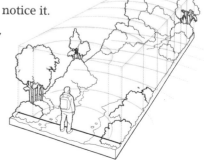

you'll find that they are easier to see if you are walking into the sun, because they cast a shadow into themselves and look deeper. Of course, if you're following a trail, you have to go in whichever direction it leads. But if you're trying to locate a track for the first time, you might find this a useful tip.

| Trail signs

Exercises like Kim's Game will help you memorize what you've seen, but before you can become an effective observer, you also need to practise seeing things in the first place. Scouts have developed a game for this that involves following a set of trail markers laid by another Scout. Each trail marker can be made in a number of ways: by scratching marks in the dirt or by setting sticks, stones or grass in a particular configuration to indicate a variety of instructions. Different people use different trail markers. Below are some suggestions.

This is the trail

Turn right (short way)

Turn left (long way)

Danger help

This way

Stop

The more you practise identifying trail markers, the better you'll become. Keep at it and you'll soon find you're able to observe markers that most people would miss.

TRACKS AND TRACKING

Tracking an animal in the wild takes real skill. You need good observational techniques, but you also need to know something about the animal you're tracking: what its tracks look like and how to follow them, how the animal behaves in the wild, and finally how to stalk it so that you can get a good look at it in its natural habitat.

Tracks

Most animals leave very distinctive tracks. Before you go out in the field, try and find out what animals you're likely to find in that particular environment and what their tracks look like. After all, there's not much point in trying to track grizzlies in England or red squirrels in the Arctic.

Eventually you'll build up your own library of tracks, but here are a few common ones to get you going.

Badger

Badger tracks are 5–8cm long. You are more likely to see claw marks on the fore paws than the back paws.

Red fox

Red fox tracks are about 5cm long. They are sometimes covered with fur, which may make them less easy to see in mud or snow.

Deer

Different varieties of deer have different footprints, but mostly they have two teardrop-shaped halves, made by their cloven hooves. They are normally 4–8cm long.

Wild boar

Wild boar tracks are normally 5–7cm long.

Beaver

A beaver's hind print is about 15cm long. Once hunted to extinction in the UK, they were reintroduced in 2005 – seeing one is a real treat.

Otter

Otter tracks can be found near waterways. In very soft ground you might see evidence of webbed feet.

Rabbit

Rabbit tracks are one of the easiest to identify because their hind paws leave a much deeper impression than their fore paws.

Squirrel

The rear paws of a squirrel resemble a human hand, having five digits that look like four fingers and a thumb. The front paw (shown) has only four digits.

Vole

Vole tracks are quite similar to squirrel tracks. They are low down the food chain, so their presence often gives you a clue that there are other animals about (see page 180).

Hare

Hares rest in the open air, so their tracks may lead you to an indentation in the ground – or form – showing you where they have been.

Hedgehog

People traditionally leave bread soaked in milk out to attract hedgehogs. Don't – they find it indigestible and it can kill them.

The quality of footprints for tracking depends a great deal on the terrain and weather conditions. The best footprints are left on a thin layer of snow or on soft ground, but many other factors affect their quality, such as what sort of soil they are left on and the speed at which the animal was moving. It's pretty rare to find absolutely clear prints: you normally have to build up a picture of the animal you're tracking from a combination of partial prints.

Having said that, a close examination of a partial print can be very enlightening. Fresh prints, for example, sometimes come up darker than older prints. If it's been raining and droplets of water are visible on the surface of the track, this indicates that the animal passed by before the rain arrived. Some very experienced trackers are able to determine the emotional state of their quarry by looking at the arrangement of the footprints: some animals will pace when they're agitated, or will show a sudden burst of speed when frightened.

When you're examining tracks, it's worth knowing that different animals have different gaits, which is to say that their footprints arrange themselves in different patterns as they walk (or run). The study of gait is an in-depth science; for tracking purposes you need to know that there are four different types of gait: the diagonal walk, the pace, the bound and the gallop. If you can recognize these different gaits, it will help you follow a track once you've found one.

Diagonal walk

This is when an animal moves one leg on each side of its body  simultaneously, i.e. right front and back left legs, then does the opposite, i.e. left front and right back. Diagonal walkers include dogs, cats and all hoofed animals.

Pace

Pacers are animals that move both limbs on one side of the body at  the same time, so they have a 'lumbering' gait. Bears, skunks, badgers and beavers are all pacers.

Bound

Bounders – such as weasels – are animals that reach out with their  front legs and pull their back legs up behind.

Gallop

All rabbits and hares gallop, and so do most rodents. Gallopers push upwards with their back feet then land on their front feet.

| Other signs

Being able to identify tracks is only half of the business of tracking. If you're on the lookout for wildlife, you need to be in tune with the natural world around you and be able to interpret the signs that your environment is giving you. Here are a few pointers.

Landscape tracking

Animals will tend to be located in 'islands' of suitable landscape; they will generally avoid the areas in between those islands unless they are simply passing through. When you're looking for an area that's suitable for animal habitation, think about what herbivores need from the land: where herbivores go, carnivores will follow.

- A good variety of vegetation will offer year-round food sources for different species.

- Water is important, though not essential as many herbivores get their water from dew or from the vegetation they eat.

- Most animals like cover to stop them from becoming a food source themselves. Open spaces are not good places to track wildlife as they provide no cover; similarly, deep forest provides little in the way of undergrowth or mixed vegetation. Your best bet for tracking is an area where two different types of landscape cross over, for example where a forest meets an open field or a stream.

- Indicator animals are creatures whose presence can lead you to deduce something else about their habitat. The presence of voles, rabbits and deer all suggest that the terrain is suitable for a wide range of species.

Signs on the ground

Tracks, of course, are one of the principle signs that an animal has passed in a particular direction, but there are others. You need a keen eye to notice some of these, but practice makes perfect!

- When pebbles lie on the ground, wind and rain will cause soil deposits to build up around them. If the pebble is kicked away by a passing animal, these deposits become visible, forming a little crater. The direction in which the pebble has been kicked gives an idea of the direction in which the animal has travelled.

- Pebbles and leaves that have been recently turned over by a passing animal will be darker in colour than those surrounding them because of moisture or soil deposits.

- If a twig or branch has been snapped, something – probably a passing animal – has applied pressure to it. You can tell if this occurred recently by finding a similar piece of wood, snapping it and comparing the breaks. Older breaks look more dull and weathered than fresh ones.

Paths

When an animal moves through tall grass or high vegetation, it will leave a path with the grass bent in the direction it travelled. Of course, it's not often that you come across a path through a field of perfect, high, virgin grass; but if you see vegetation bent at an angle, perhaps damaged in some way, it can be an indication that an animal has passed by.

After dew, rain or frost, you can often see the path an animal has taken even if you can't see its actual footprints – the path it left will show up as a dark line on the ground.

Most individual creatures have paths or runs that they frequently follow, and in thick forest these paths are often the animals' only means of getting about. They are sometimes shared with other animals and are used day and night to guide the animal or to allow it to run away. Follow the path and, if you're lucky, you might find the animal somewhere along the way.

Animal paths are usually most distinct around feeding areas and water sources. If you come across small paths joining to create a larger path, the larger path often leads to water: stalking the water source is a good way of getting a glimpse of the animal.

Animals often leave telltale tracks through high grass.

Urine and faeces

It might sound unpleasant, but an animal's defecating habits and deposits can be a big help when you're tracking them. It's said that there are trackers who are able to identify the presence of different animals by recognizing the smell of their urine on the breeze. That's pretty advanced stuff. However, animal droppings – or scat, as they are technically called – are a very good means of telling whether and how recently an animal has passed, though it should be said that an animal's droppings can differ quite widely depending on what it has eaten and its state of health.

In general, though, different animals have different-shaped droppings. Herbivore droppings tend to be small and round; carnivore droppings are often more sausage-shaped. The following list should help you identify some of them:

- Tube-shaped: dog family, skunks, raccoons, bears

- Tube-shaped and tapered at one end: foxes

- Tear-shaped, tapered at one end: cat family

- Pellet-shaped: rabbits and hares

- Oblong, with a teat shape at the end: deer

- Very thin tubes, like the lead of a pencil: rodents

Herbivores have to eat a lot more food than carnivores, so they produce more droppings. Sometimes animals will use their faeces to mark out their territory. If this is the case, they might lay them above the ground – on a tree stump, for example – so that their odour is more easily disseminated.

Some creatures – notably badgers in the UK and raccoons in the US – create dedicated latrines where there will be a large quantity of droppings. If you come

HIDDEN DANGERS

Animal droppings can be germ ridden. Some experts examine them by touch, in which case they always wear protective gloves. Most examination is done by sight, however. When the droppings are old and dry, they sometimes give off a dust that can cause disease, so when you're examining them, make sure you stand upwind.

across a fresh animal latrine, you can be sure that the animals will return to that place.

The state of an animal's droppings can give you an indication as to how recently the animal passed. Fresh droppings are wetter and often attract flies; as they get older, they dry out, become smaller and are of less interest as an insect food source!

Feeding signs

As animals travel, they eat. If you can learn to observe feeding signs, you'll find that they can provide almost as good a trail as footprints in the earth. But feeding signs can be difficult to spot. The more you track, the more you will come to recognize them. Deer, for example, having no top incisor teeth, have to grip on the vegetation and tear it from the stalk. This leaves a telltale frayed end. Rabbits, on the other hand, clip the vegetation very finely.

Feeding signs are the kind of thing that a person untrained in observation will easily miss, but if you examine the vegetation around you carefully, you'll be amazed what it can tell you.

Animal homes

The best place to spot an animal, of course, is near its home, but before you can do that you need to know something of its habits and habitats. The easiest homes to spot are birds' nests but, as you become a skilled observer, you'll find many more.

Some animals, such as foxes, badgers and rabbits, dig holes, or warrens, in which to live. Just because you've come across an animal hole, however, doesn't mean it's occupied. Most animals tend to move quite regularly, unless they are birthing or hibernating. Examining the area around the animal hole will give you an idea of whether it's in use. For example, if there are cobwebs over the hole, accumulated leaves or overgrown vegetation, these are good indications that it's unused; whereas fresh feeding signs or droppings

Home is a great place to find a particular animal – but observe from a distance.

in the vicinity are good indications that the hole is active. It's not unusual for certain animals, such as foxes and badgers, to use the same hole, so don't be surprised if you see contradictory signs around it.

Other animals, such as deer or hares, sleep on thick beds of vegetation in well-camouflaged positions. You can sometimes find depressions in the vegetation forming the shape of the animal that has lain there, as well as nearby droppings and feeding signs. Squirrels make nests up trees not unlike birds' nests.

I remember once in the US coming across a place, deep in a thicket in a remote forest, where a pride of mountain lions had been laying up. The grass was all flattened and the air thick with their scent. I have experienced this a few times and it is an amazing, heart-thumping moment where you enter into the animal world for a privileged insight into their real existence. You can almost sense their raw power and it feels like you are on borrowed time, as if you are witnessing something forbidden to humans. Likewise, I once climbed inside a dark, dank pit under the roots of a tree that was the home of a 5-metre python (who was luckily out!). I sensed the hairs on the back of my neck rise as I lay in the indentations and depressions in the earth where this frightening, formidable predator had only recently laid. This is the magic of tracking wild animals.

Hair tracks

As animals brush past bushes and low branches, they sometimes leave clumps of hair. As you become a more expert tracker, you'll start to recognize different animal hairs; in the meantime you'll get a clue as to what animal it belongs depending on how high it is from the ground. Hair found a metre from the ground, for example, is more likely to come from a deer than a fox.

Fur balls on barbed wire indicate an animal has passed by.

Using your ears

Animals are adept at not being seen. If you can train your ears as well as your eyes, it will add a whole new dimension to your tracking skills. Hunters in certain parts of Africa know this better than most. They must recognize the sounds lions make when they are hunting, feeding, mating or looking after their cubs: stumbling across a lion when it's doing one of these things is very bad for your health!

TRAINING EXERCISES

In everyday life we're not used to focusing our hearing, but it is something we can teach ourselves. Ask someone to hide a ticking wristwatch in a completely dark room. With your sight disabled, you need to focus your hearing on the sound of the watch in order to find it.

The bark of a fox or the bleat of a deer will alert you to their presence; but so can the noise of a branch breaking underfoot, the rustling of tall grass or a bush and the sound of water splashing. Tune your ears in to the sound of the wild and you will be much more aware of what is going on around you.

STALKING

When you're trying to see an animal in its natural habitat, following its trail is only half the battle. Wild animals live a precarious existence, avoiding predators as they go about the business of survival. In most parts of the world, of course, the top predator – the one all animals want to avoid – is man. They will use all their cunning to keep away from us. In turn, we must use all *our* cunning to stalk them.

Stalking is the act of observing an animal without being observed yourself; of being able to move without being seen; and of knowing how to camouflage yourself. When we are trailing and stalking, we use our sight, hearing and, sometimes, our sense of smell. So too do animals. We need to keep this in mind if we want to get a glimpse of them.

If what you're observing can kill you, double the distance and be especially vigilant.

Generally speaking, animals are at their most active at dawn and dusk. So, get up early, follow the tips in this section and you'll massively improve your chances of seeing wildlife in its natural habitat.

How not to be seen

When we're trying not to be seen, we have to remember why things *are* seen: shape, shadow, silhouette, surface, spacing and movement (see pages 173–4). All these attributes make us visible. When we're stalking animals, we have three weapons in our arsenal to counteract them: camouflage, cover and stealth.

Camouflage

Most mammals are colour blind. This means that they determine shapes around them according to contrast – the difference between dark patches, light patches and the various shades of grey in between. Imagine you could only see in black and white. If you looked at someone dressed all in the same colour who was standing against a varied background, you would see

Stealth: one of the best weapons you have in your arsenal.

IMPROVISING IN THE FIELD

The skin of your face is an easily seen surface. You can break up the surface and make it blend into the background by applying camouflage stripes. Specialized army camouflage paint sticks are available, but they're not really necessary. A piece of burnt wood from your campfire will mark your skin sufficiently. With camo on the face, less is more. Your aim is to break up the human shape and monotone colour, not simply to replace one light colour with one mud colour!

a very definite human shape. Now, imagine the person you are watching was wearing patches of different colours. The shape of their body would be broken up – it would look less human.

When we're stalking animals, therefore, the best way to camouflage ourselves is to wear clothing that breaks up blocks of colour. Army camouflage gear is good for this, but it's by no means necessary. You can achieve the same effect by making sure, for example, that your trousers and your top are of substantially different shades. Wearing knee patches will break up the shape of your legs, and patterned cloth is better than cloth of one colour. If you can include some shades on your clothing that will help you blend into the background (browns and greens, for example, in a forest), so much the better. Breaking up the colours, however, is the most important thing.

If the sun is shining, you need to make sure it can't reflect off anything that you have about you. Cameras and binoculars are the worst culprits, but even the metallic buckle on a rucksack can glint in the sunlight, as can a watch face or metal strap. I remember seeing one US soldier sneaking around all camo-ed up to the nines, with foliage sticking out of everywhere, but with his glaring gold wristwatch and strap in full view like a traffic light! It might seem like a small thing to you, but to a wild animal (or a hunted soldier) it's an effective warning sign.

Cover

Cover is as important for the stalker as it is for the soldier. Just as someone on the front line will shun open ground in case they reveal themselves to the enemy, so a stalker needs to use the natural cover of his or her terrain to avoid being seen. Here are a few tips for making good use of natural cover:

- Avoid the skyline. Nothing will announce your presence quite like silhouetting yourself against the horizon. Walking up on the horizon of ridgelines is especially dangerous.

- Crouch behind bushes so that most of your body is hidden.

- In grass that offers very little cover you should crawl. Learning how to crawl is an art in itself (see opposite).

- Make use of undulating ground. If the terrain in front of you heads upwards, this will cover you from anything over the brow of the hill – provided any potential observers don't move, of course. Don't be afraid to duck down in a ditch if it's going to give you good cover.

- Even if you're wearing good, patchy camouflage, try and stick to areas where the colours you are wearing blend in to the background. Remember that camo is no use against a plain, white wall!

HIDE LIKE THIS NOT LIKE THIS

At some point during a stalk you will find yourself hiding in a static position behind an object, whether it's a tree, a bush or a boulder. If this is the case, you need to ensure that whatever part of your body is visible blends in with the shape of the object that's concealing you. So much of the skill of stalking, especially as you draw near your prey, is about blending in cleverly with and adapting to your cover.

Stealth

Animals in the wild are extremely sensitive to movement. The less you move the more chance you'll have of seeing them. Even if you don't follow any of the other principles of tracking and stalking, you need to follow this one.

We would endlessly practise different crawling techniques in the military.

Keep moving in a forest and I guarantee you'll see almost nothing. But if you sit still – *really* still – and wait, sooner or later something will amble across your path. Immobile, you're far more difficult to see. Even if you *can* be seen, animals will perceive that you are much less of a threat if you're not moving. If you have to move, do so slowly – centimetre by centimetre. Sudden movements are the worst, and will scare away anything that sees them.

In the military, soldiers are taught techniques of individual movement, including some military-specific crawls. It's worth learning a couple of these – they'll make you a lot stealthier in the field.

The *leopard crawl*: to perform this manoeuvre, get down on your knees and forearms. Move your right elbow forward with your left knee, then vice versa.

The *stomach crawl*: lying on your stomach with your arms in front of you and your legs splayed out with your heels on the ground. Pull with your forearms while pushing with the inside of your feet.

Sometimes you just can't help being seen by the animal you're stalking. If that happens, freeze. By remaining absolutely still you increase your chance of blending into the background and reduce the risk of the animal seeing you as a threat. I have often spotted a deer in the woods and, although I've been out in the open, the deer has not seen me. This is because I have stopped and frozen, and the deer did not notice me. Stillness in the wild (and in life in general) is a great lesson to learn. My grandfather used to say to me, 'There is always music in the garden, but you have to be quiet enough to hear it.'

BEAR'S SECRET SCOUTING TIPS

There are two quick ways to tell which way the wind is blowing. Wet all around one finger with your tongue and then hold it up into the air. Whichever side is coldest indicates the direction from which the wind is coming. Alternatively, throw some dust or dried grass in the air and watch how it falls.

How not to be smelled

We all stink – at least we do to most creatures. Animals have a much more acute sense of smell than humans – you only have to see a bloodhound on the trail to realize that. This highly developed sense of smell is a primary defence mechanism. If an animal smells you – and they will if you're not careful – they'll run. When you're stalking, therefore, you need to be very aware of the wind. It will carry your scent easily. Move *against* the wind. If that's not possible, try and get yourself into a position where you are crosswind from the animal. Never approach a creature from downwind if you want it to stick around. Remember, some animals can smell you from a mile away. Think of the polar bear – the male can smell the female from 145 kilometres away! You're not operating against humans here: your adversary is highly tuned and highly sensitive. To win, you need to learn to think like the animal and you need to understand their powers. But also remember their limitations – it is because of these that you, with the superior brain, can win.

How not to be heard

Animals have very good hearing – they need to, in order to tell if predators are approaching. Sound is caused by vibration. As we walk, our footsteps cause the ground to vibrate like a drum and animals can pick up on this. (Snakes even manage to 'hear' without having an outer ear. By resting their jaw on the ground they can pick up the vibrations of anything passing nearby.)

I remember once walking with a veteran Selous Scout, once the most feared counter-insurgency force on the African continent. They were expert man-trackers and masters of bushcraft. He told me that with snakes, the worst position to be in a patrol was number three. The first man wakes the snake up with his vibrations, the second man makes the snake mad and the third man gets bitten. (That's worth remembering!) He also showed me an old bushcraft trick for picking up vibrations from far away. Stick your knife into the ground and put your ear up to the handle. The metal will act as an amplifier and you'll be able to hear footsteps in the distance much more easily.

When stalking an animal, you need to make sure they're not alerted to the sound of your presence by your footsteps. This means walking quietly. Most people are flat-footed when they walk, slamming their sole against the ground. To walk quietly, change this technique according to the terrain.

On grass/leaves

Let your heel touch the ground first and then slowly roll your feet down to your toe. Balance on your back foot as the other probes forward, ready to take the weight gently on its heel as the new lead foot.

On rocky/hard ground

Step with your toe first. Make sure you have a solid footing that is not going to dislodge any stones and make a noise and then gently bring down your heel. Again, you should balance on your back foot until the front one can take the weight.

Your footsteps are not the only noises that could give you away. Be aware of any bushes around you – brushing against them, no matter how gently, can cause a warning alarm for the animal you're stalking. So move branches aside carefully and gently, replacing them behind you as you move. The Embera tribe in Central America, with whom I trained, talked about 'becoming' like a tiger, moving slinkily (if that is a word!) through the foliage.

BINOCULARS AND TELESCOPES

These can be useful when you can't get close enough to view an animal properly. However, you should first locate it with your naked eye: trying to find something through a viewing device is more difficult because the magnification reduces your field of vision. Our peripheral vision is much better at spotting movement. Overuse of binos can also give you eye strain.

HIDES AND OBSERVATION POSTS

We've seen that movement is a crucial giveaway when you don't want to be seen. It's very difficult, however, to stay perfectly still for long periods of time. A hide or observation post puts a screen between yourself and what you're observing, a barrier that allows you to move relatively freely without being spotted and alarming the animals you are watching. They are not really needed for short-term observation when you can rely on your own ability to stay still; but for long-term stake-outs, they're invaluable.

A simple hide can be made from natural materials found in the forest, such as foliage, long grass and branches. More often, however, people take hide-building materials

Home sweet home for me in the swamps!

with them. These are made from old army surplus camouflage nets or hessian sack material painted in camouflage colours and to which cut-up bits of material have been attached to break up the outline. These are either suspended from branches and the surrounding bushes or from collapsible tent-type poles.

Whatever materials you use, you need to leave small holes, or 'ports', through which you can observe your quarry. A pair of secateurs is useful so you can silently snip away foliage to allow better observation of the area.

SEEING AT NIGHT

One of the best ways of spotting animals is to stalk at night; but, of course, night-time observation presents its own set of issues.

In order to understand how our night vision works, we need to learn something about the eye. The back of our eye is covered with two different types of cells: cones and rods. The cones are responsible for seeing detail and colour; the rods are responsible for peripheral vision, movement and seeing in dim light.

The rods contain a chemical called rhodopsin. Rhodopsin allows our eyes to perceive light. When we view things in dim light, it's the rhodopsin in our rod

BEAR'S SECRET SCOUTING TIPS

The rod cells that contain rhodopsin are located around the edge of the eye. This means that our peripheral vision is better at seeing in dim light than our direct vision. Consequently, at night, you see objects better and will be more aware of shapes and movements if you don't look directly at them, but look slightly off to one side. Try it.

cells that lets us do this. Bright light, however, bleaches the chemical, making it less effective in darker conditions. It takes about thirty minutes for the bleaching effect to dissipate, though most of this occurs in the first ten minutes. This is why, when you switch your light out at night, it takes about ten minutes for your 'night vision' to establish itself. Switching the light back on will bleach the rhodopsin and cause temporary night blindness.

Rhodopsin is less sensitive to red light than to white light. This means that if you use a torch with a red light to see in the dark, it will not cause your night vision to deteriorate in the same way as using a white light. (This is why soldiers in the field use red torches at night.) If you do have to use a white light at night, covering one eye with your hand will stop the rhodopsin in that eye from bleaching, so preserving half of your night vision. As soldiers, if we had to use white light, we would cover the face of the torch with tape and make pin-prick holes in it to reduce the light spread and focus it on whatever we needed to see close-up. This, again, minimized night-vision loss.

Night-viewing devices

Once your natural night vision has become accustomed to the dark, you should be able to see quite well. There are, however, instruments that will increase the effectiveness of your night vision.

Binoculars

Binoculars are much underrated as a night-viewing device when there is some ambient light source (the moon perhaps, or the stars). If you can see something in the dark, a pair of binoculars will magnify it just as effectively as they would do in the day.

Certain binoculars are better for night-time and low-light observation. Every set of binoculars has two numbers written on the case – 8x50, for example. The first number indicates the level of magnification. The second number is the objective lens width. This tells you how much light the binoculars let in. The higher this second number, the better the binoculars are for low-light viewing. (The first number should not be too high, because although the magnification will be better, the field of view will become smaller and the binoculars will become sensitive to every movement of your hand. Anything above 8 is only really suitable if you can fix your binoculars to a tripod.) Maritime binoculars, which have very wide objective lenses, are particularly good for night-time viewing.

Night-vision devices

Night-vision devices (or NVDs) aren't just the preserve of the SAS – civvies can get their hands on them too, though they don't come cheap.

NVDs work by intensifying available light sources. This means that they will allow you to see in the dark provided there is some ambient light. They will also pick up infrared light. This means that if there *isn't* any natural light, you can flood the area with infrared – invisible to the human eye and to the eyes of *most* animals. (In the military, they use infrared flares to light up huge areas of terrain at night without benefiting the enemy, then scan the area using NV.) You can easily make such a light by taping an infrared filter (available from photography shops) over your torch, but most NV sights have their own integral infrared light source.

Modern NV is much better than earlier generations of the technology. NV generation 4 gives a much sharper image and better depth of field, but it is extremely expensive. You can buy NV generation 1 devices much more reasonably (look on eBay). If you manage to get your hands on one, use it to look at the stars at night. I can guarantee you an amazing experience!

Thermal imaging

Thermal image intensifiers – much used by the military and the fire service – are also very expensive. They work by detecting the heat emanating from an animal or target. Thermal imaging devices have two advantages over NV: they don't require *any* ambient light source, and they will 'look' through solid matter such as bushes. In the military they are used to locate sentries who are camouflaged and still, which isn't very different from what you're doing when you stalk an animal at night.

The only thing that will defeat thermal imaging devices is glass, which has its own thermal profile.

RECORDING NATURE

If you see an amazing sight in the natural world, chances are you'll want to record it. Modern camera technology makes this easy.

Cameras

Digital cameras are great in the field because you don't have to lug loads of film about. You can get very compact ones, which have the benefit of not taking up much space but compromise somewhat on quality. At the other end of the scale are digital SLR cameras that allow you to fix additional lenses. These are better suited for wildlife photography, but they're bigger, bulkier and more expensive. The more you get into recording nature, the more you'll want to experiment with these better cameras; but when you're starting out, the compact designs will still give you excellent results. Remember: the person who can get up close and personal to an animal will always get the better picture, no matter what equipment they're using. Good stalking techniques are worth a thousand fancy camera lenses.

Digiscopes

Digiscoping kits allow you to attach your digital camera to a telescope, so you can take very high-quality photographs of an animal that you might be viewing from quite a distance.

Camcorders

There is a wide range of compact, high-quality camcorders available. MiniDV cameras are very popular: they take decent digital images and record them on to very small tapes – it's easy to fit a couple of these into your pack.

The quality of photographs taken with even the smallest of digital cameras can be quite incredible – and might even win you some prizes!

Tracking and stalking are taught in the military from day one. In the Special Forces they are skills that are honed to perfection. Many people think of the SAS as being primarily a fighting force, but in fact its main role is reconnaissance. A patrol needs to move silently, observe without being observed and accurately record what it sees. These skills are vital to the success of most military operations.

As with all things related to scouting and fieldcraft, you never stop learning, as a friend of mine with over 30 years experience found out when he was tracking in Africa. He was with some incredibly skilled soldiers from the Venda and Zulu tribes. These locals had been tracking all their lives, sometimes to put food on the table, sometimes operationally during the South African Bushwar. They had an amazing amount of knowledge, and they were passing on their skills to my friend.

One day, they were tracking a small group of barefoot soldiers when the trail took them into a local village. The villagers also went barefoot, and goats and cattle were given free rein to walk around the dusty streets. As you can imagine, singling out the footprints of the men they were tracking was incredibly difficult among the multitude of human, goat and cattle tracks. My friend looked at his companions, but to his surprise, they just smiled at him, said it was up to him to sort it out and went to drink tea with the locals.

Determined not to be beaten and relishing the chance to show off his new skills, he started casting in bigger and bigger circles. Every time he thought he had located the trail, he got down on to his hands and knees among the goat and cow pooh to try to follow the signs. They always petered out into a mass of conflicting tracks.

Eventually, after thirty minutes of watching (and laughing), his African colleagues approached to see how he was getting on. Frustrated and rather smelly from crawling around in all the dirt, he had to admit that he hadn't found a single conclusive track. 'Don't worry,' he was told. 'It will be over here.' The Africans led him straight to the soldiers' tracks where they had left the village.

My friend had just learned a valuable lesson in a technique known as 'car parking'. This is where, if there are either too many confusing tracks, or not enough (as you might expect if your trail led you into a tarmac car park), there's no point trying to find the individual track. Instead, you use common sense to work out which way your quarry would have left. If you have been following them for a while, you should have a general sense of the direction in which they're heading. So, if they entered an area from the north, they probably left from the south. And this is exactly what the soldiers had done.

Try and get inside the head of your quarry and you'll find things suddenly become a whole lot easier. And remember that common sense and the ability to read between the lines are the most important attributes in a good tracker.

FIELD
FIRST AID
AND RESCUE

the skills of managing injury, paramedic style!

Rigorous simulated training exercises such as this one are an essential part of any SAS medic's training.

Good medical training is crucial in the field. In a four-man SAS patrol, one member will generally be a medic. SAS medics go through a rigorous training procedure, including a period in an actual hospital. The medic is an essential member of any SAS patrol, and I don't just say that because I was trained as one! He'll know how to treat wounds, counter infections, deal with gunshot trauma and all the other emergency first aid issues that can emerge whenever an SAS patrol is carrying out its work. But what if the medic comes to harm? The remainder of the patrol would have to look after him, and themselves. So, all SAS troopers have to have a basic level of field-expedient first aid knowledge. (In a senior patrol, there will probably be more than one medic as everyone ends up learning most of the major skills.)

HIDDEN DANGERS

If there's more than one person wounded, working out who needs attention the most urgently is a very difficult process. It's tempting to go to the one who's screaming the loudest; but if someone's screaming, that's actually a pretty good sign. At least it means they're conscious and breathing! The quiet patients are often the ones you need to worry about the most: it's the unconscious, non-breathing victim who needs your attention, and fast. So don't get distracted by the noise and chaos of an emergency – keep focused. The training we received in the SAS for emergency trauma management was as close to the real thing as you can get, to the extent that it was almost impossible to tell if the injury was genuine or not – the actors, pumping blood, smoke and noise were very realistic. But training like this teaches you to think clearly in an emergency, and clear, fast thinking, saves lives.

Similarly, out in the wild, you can't rely on someone else having the know-how to administer treatment in the event of a medical emergency. You need to be able to do it yourself, because even the most experienced fieldcraft expert can come unstuck in unfamiliar terrain and the chances are you're going to be a long way from the nearest doctor. A working knowledge of field-expedient first aid could save someone's life. It could even save your own.

However, if someone on your trip sustains a serious injury, particularly a head injury, it is essential that you immediately seek professional medical help.

Basic first aid kit

For any trip out into the field, it is essential to carry a basic first aid kit. Yours should contain the following items:

- A selection of assorted sized plasters
- 2–3 sterile wound dressings (these have a sterile dressing pad attached to a bandage; if you can't find these then get sterile pads and separate bandages)
- Roller bandages (the self-adhesive type are the best as you don't need to carry safety pins)
- Triangular bandages (good for slings and even dressings)
- Tweezers, for removing splinters
- Blister plasters
- Painkillers, such as paracetamol or aspirin (remember to adhere to the dosage rates as analgesics are potentially harmful and do not give aspirin to anyone under the age of 16)
- Alcohol-free wipes for cleaning around wounds
- Alcohol gel (to clean your hands)
- A pair of disposable non-latex gloves

Useful extras
- A syringe
- Roll of cling film and/or clean plastic bags (for use as a burns dressing)

COLLAPSED CASUALTY

If a person collapses the first thing you must do is assess whether or not he or she is unconscious. Talk to them and ask them if they are all right. If there's no response, shake their shoulders firmly. If there's still no reaction they are unconscious.

Your next task is to find out if they're breathing. If the casualty is unconscious and lying on his or her back, the muscles in their throat and neck will relax and the tongue will fall back and block the air passages that lead to the lungs. So, kneel by the person's head, put one hand on their forehead and tilt their head back. Put two fingers of your other hand underneath their chin and lift it. This will pull the tongue away from the back of the throat. Put your ear as near to the

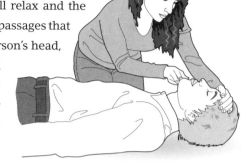

person's mouth and nose as you can, listening and feeling for breaths against your cheek. At the same time, look along the chest to see if it is moving.

Breathing casualty

If the casualty is breathing, place them on their side in what's known as the recovery position. This position will keep the airways clear, so that they can continue to breathe, and allow fluid and mucus to drain easily from their mouth, preventing choking. Likewise, if they vomit while unconscious, it will drain away. Check the person's pulse. Using your index and middle finger of one hand, feel around the underside of the wrist until you find the pulse. Alternatively, press the same two fingers against one side of the

TRAINING EXERCISES

Like everything in this chapter, it's a good idea to make sure you know how to get someone into the recovery position before you go out into the field. Luckily, this is very easy to practise. Make sure the patient is lying down on their back. Kneel down beside them. Place the arm nearest you at right angles to the body and bring the other one across their body so that the palm of their hand is against the side of their face that's nearest you. Bend the furthest leg at the knee and bring it up until the foot is flat on the floor. Holding the casualty's furthest shoulder and the knee, pull the bent knee towards you until they are on their side. Adjust the leg that's now uppermost so that the hip and knee are at right angles to each other (to stop the patient rolling forward). Make sure the head is tilted back and that medical help is on the way.

RECOVERY POSITION

patient's neck, just beneath the jaw. Count how many beats you feel in a full minute – an adult's normal resting heart rate is between 60 and 100 beats per minute.

Non-breathing casualty

If the patient is not breathing, then you will need to give them cardiopulmonary resuscitation (CPR; see below). Ask someone to call for emergency help while you start CPR. If you are on your own and the casualty is an adult, call for help first then begin CPR. If the casualty is a child give CPR for one minute, call for help and then continue with CPR.

CARDIOPULMONARY RESUSCITATION (CPR)

It can be very scary when someone stops breathing. As soon as the human body stops breathing, it is minutes away from death unless someone administers appropriate first aid. Once breathing stops the heart will also stop, as it is no longer being supplied with oxygen, and the longer the body is without oxygen the more long-term damage it's likely to sustain. Keep calm, and act swiftly and decisively. You could save a life by maintaining circulation with chest compressions and by delivering oxygen into the body with rescue breaths – together these techniques are called cardiopulmonary resuscitation or CPR. All soldiers are trained to do this.

In an adult, chest compressions are performed first because it is most likely that breathing has stopped because of a problem with the heart.

Chest compressions for adults

With your patient on their back, kneel at their side level with their chest. Lay the heel of one hand on the centre of the chest where the two halves of the ribcage meet. Put your other hand on top and interlock your fingers to stop yourself performing the compressions with anything other than the heel of your hand (keep your fingers well clear of their chest). Kneel upright directly over the chest and press down so the ribcage sinks 4–5cm, then release the pressure without taking your hands away. Repeat to give 30 compressions.

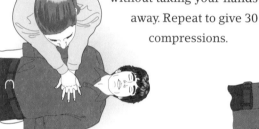

Rescue breaths for adults

This technique is used to get the air flowing back into the lungs of someone who has stopped breathing. There are a number of reasons why this might have happened, including electric shock and inhalation of water or smoke.

Move up nearer the patient's head. Tilt their head back and lift their chin to open the airway again. With one hand pinch the patient's nostrils shut. Take a normal breath and place your mouth firmly over the patient's mouth. Try to make sure there are no air gaps. Now blow into their lungs until the chest rises (it should take about one second). Take your mouth away and watch the chest fall. Take another breath and repeat for a second time.

Continue the sequence of 30 chest compressions followed by two rescue breaths until the person starts to breathe normally, help arrives or you are too exhausted to continue. If the person starts to breathe normally again, roll them over into the recovery position (see pages 202–3). If the patient regains consciousness, they'll probably be very agitated. Keep them warm and calm them by explaining clearly what has happened.

CPR for children

The procedure for children is slightly different. If a child is unconscious and their breathing stops, it is most likely to be caused by a breathing difficulty rather than a heart problem, so you begin CPR by giving the patient five rescue breaths. After that you revert to the cycle of 30 chest compressions followed by two rescue breaths.

The steps for giving rescue breaths to a child are essentially the same as for adults. Tilt the head to lift the chin, pinch the nostrils closed and breathe into the mouth until the chest rises. Watch it fall and repeat to give up to *five* breaths. Then give chest compressions. Place one hand only on the centre of the child's chest. Keep your fingers raised, kneel over the child and depress the chest by about one-third of its depth. Give 30 compressions, followed by *two* more rescue breaths. As for adults, keep going until the child starts to breathe normally, medical help arrives or you are too tired to keep going.

CHOKING

Choking normally occurs when something – usually food – obstructs the entrance to the windpipe. If you suspect this is happening, ask the patient if they are choking.

HIDDEN DANGERS

Emergency resuscitation techniques are not a replacement for proper medical care, which you should seek out immediately. If the patient starts breathing normally, keep them under close observation until medical help arrives – you may need to start CPR again if they relapse. *Never leave the patient alone.*

TRAINING EXERCISE

Chest compressions and rescue breaths are not the kind of things you want to be doing for the first time in a real-life situation. You should practise on a dummy or doll (never on a person who is breathing), along with a friend – preferably someone who's going out into the field with you. There are lots of first aid courses, such as those run by the St John Ambulance, the Red Cross or the St Andrew's Ambulance in Scotland. It's worth your while going on one of these – these are skills that you could need at any time, and in any walk of life.

If they can speak, cough and breathe in response to you, encourage them to cough up the cause of the problem. If they can only reply using hand gestures, you will need to help remove whatever is causing the obstruction.

There are two ways to do this. First try slapping the person's back. Make them lean forward so that gravity can help, then use the heel of your hand to give them five sharp blows between the shoulder blades. Check the mouth to see if the obstruction has come out. If the blockage is still there, you need to use a technique called abdominal thrusts. Stand behind the person, wrap your arms around their waist and get them to lean forward. Clench one hand and lay it against their upper abdomen, halfway between the belly button and the breastbone. Place your other hand on top of your first and then pull your hands into the patient's stomach using a sharp, upward movement up to five times. Check the mouth again.

Repeat the back slaps and abdominal thrusts up to three times (check the mouth between each set). If the person is still choking, call for medical help, repeat the cycle until the blockage is expelled, help arrives or the person becomes unconscious.

WOUND CARE

Don't ignore any wound, no matter how small. In the wild, the smallest cut can lead to infection; so can larger wounds, though these present the added problem of blood loss, which can be life threatening.

Preventing infection

Infection occurs when a wound becomes contaminated by bacteria, which can multiply at an alarming rate. Bacteria can be introduced when the wound occurs, through the use of non-sterile equipment or dressings, or on account of dirty hands. Keeping things clean and sterile in the field is not easy, and if the wound is serious then your primary concern is to control the bleeding. If time allows, however, you should try and do the following before administering treatment:

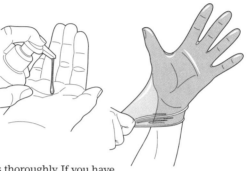

* Wash your hands thoroughly. If you have alcohol cleaning gel with you, use that, as it will kill most of the bacteria on your skin. Put on disposable gloves if you have them.

* Rinse a dirty wound under clean running water. If the water is dirty you may be able to sterilize it. This can be done by boiling it for a minute at sea level, plus an extra minute for every 300 metres above sea level. Leave it to cool completely before using it.

* If you don't have a sterile dressing you can use a folded piece of cloth, or even a triangular bandage. Hold it by its corners, open it out and, without touching the centre, refold it so that the clean inner surface faces outwards. Place it on the wound.

Minor wounds

If the bleeding is not severe, the wound should be washed. Remove any clothing around it, and then thoroughly clean the whole area. Flood the wound with water to remove any loose debris. Don't try to pick out anything that is stuck in the wound. Pat the area dry and cover with a sterile dressing. If you suspect there is anything left in the wound then summon medical help to inspect it.

Serious external bleeding

External bleeding can be divided into three types: capillary bleeding, venous bleeding (from the veins) and arterial bleeding (from the arteries). Serious wounds often contain a combination of these.

Capillary bleeding is what you get from a minor cut or scrape. It is characterized by a slow ooze of blood that clots easily. You can sterilize the wound as above and apply a dressing to stop it from becoming infected, but the bleeding will usually stop fairly quickly, especially if you apply pressure to the wound.

Venous bleeding presents a slow, steady flow of darker red blood. Pressure in the veins is not very high, but venous bleeding can be quite severe. It's generally easier to control, however, than arterial bleeding. The arteries carry blood *away* from the heart under high pressure; so arterial bleeding is characterized by brighter red blood that comes in spurts in time with the beating of the patient's heart. If arterial bleeding is severe, you don't have time to mess around. When a large artery is severed, loss of blood can cause death in less than five minutes if it is not controlled. A first aider cannot replace blood in the field, but you can attempt to control it while someone goes for help.

If there is a lot of blood from arterial or venous bleeding, you should always prioritize stopping the bleeding over cleaning the injury. Severe blood loss means that fluid is lost from the person's blood circulation, which causes shock (see page 210–11). There are four important steps to take to control bleeding, which should be carried out in the following order.

Apply direct pressure

Quickly expose the wound and place a sterile dressing or clean cloth over it. Press against the wound. If neither of these is available, or you can't get to them quickly enough, apply pressure with your hand. The pressure needs to continue, firm and even, until the bleeding stops. You should avoid releasing the pressure to see if the blood is still flowing. Keep the pressure on for about thirty minutes. In most instances, this will be long enough for the blood to stop.

IMPROVISING IN THE FIELD

Infections are more likely to be caused by debris in the wound than by unsterilized water, so if that's all you have, use it to irrigate the wound. If you have no water to hand, or supplies are low, fresh urine will perform the same function. I know... don't say it!

BEAR'S SECRET SCOUTING TIPS

A pair of disposable (non-latex) gloves and a syringe are useful additions to your first aid pack – the gloves for keeping your dirty hands away from the wound, the syringe for washing it.

Raise the wound

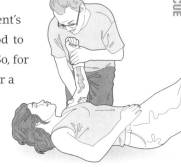

Raise the injury so that it is above the level of the patient's heart; if you do this it will take longer for the blood to reach the injury, which will help stem the bleeding. So, for a scalp wound sit the person up slightly; for an arm or a leg injury – as long as you are sure there are no bones broken – simply hold the injured limb up. Elevation is not enough on its own, however – it must be accompanied by direct pressure.

Lay the person down

Stop the patient moving around. Lie them down on a coat or insulating material to protect them from the cold ground. Keeping the injury raised (you may need help at this point), raise and support the legs to keep as much blood as possible in the core of the body, which keeps the vital organs such as the heart, lungs and brain, supplied.

Bandage the dressing in place

To help maintain the pressure, secure the pad with a bandage. If the dressing becomes saturated with blood, don't remove it, but put another dressing on top of the first one. If the second dressing is soaked with blood you are probably not applying pressure over the correct point so remove both dressings and start again. Make sure that medical help is on the way.

Abdominal wounds

These are slightly different to other wounds in that cleaning them can often introduce more infection than it avoids. Should any of the internal organs be showing, don't try to push them back in. Cover them with cling film, if you have some, to prevent them drying out. Cover this with a dressing pad. The patient will naturally tend to adopt whichever position is most comfortable for them – this will often be lying down with knees bent slightly to ease the strain on the abdomen. Let them do so. Make sure that someone is getting emergency medical help.

INTERNAL BLEEDING

This is quite difficult to diagnose, but if a patient is bleeding profusely from the nose or mouth, it could be a sign of internal bleeding. Other symptoms include nausea, a weak, rapid pulse, thirst, paleness and lack of energy – but these are also signs of shock (see below). If you suspect internal bleeding, it's important to get medical attention immediately, but in the meantime you should treat the patient as follows:

- Lie the patient flat on their back on a blanket or coat.

- If the patient needs to vomit, get them to turn their head to one side.

- Keep the patient warm, but do not use a hot water bottle or lay the patient near a fire.

- If the patient is unconscious, check their breathing (see page 202). If they are still breathing, lay them on their side in the recovery position (see pages 202–3). This will keep their airways clear, help them to breathe unaided and support their chest. It will also enable them to vomit without difficulty.

SHOCK

There are two kinds of shock. Psychological shock is a mental reaction to bad news or trauma. It can be serious and long lasting. In the field, however, you need to be prepared to encounter life-threatening physiological shock, which is a very distinct medical issue.

Shock occurs when the circulatory system fails and is not able to deliver sufficient oxygen around the body. The most likely reasons for this happening in the field are as a result of fluids being lost from internal or external bleeding, burns, severe diarrhoea and/or vomiting. Your priority should be to treat the underlying cause, but you need to be vigilant for the signs of shock, which are:

- ❋ Drained appearance

- ❋ Cold, pale, clammy skin, which will eventually go blue-grey as oxygen levels drop

- ❋ Shallow breathing

- ❋ Weak, rapid pulse

- ❋ Excessive yawning or sighing

- ❋ Nausea or vomiting

- ❋ Severe thirst, lack of energy

- ❋ In extreme cases, the person will start gasping for air and may become unconscious. If not treated then their heart might stop.

If you suspect that your patient is suffering from shock you should, unless their injuries prevent it, lie them down on a blanket or coat and raise their legs. Cover them with a coat or blanket to keep them warm, but do not place them near a fire or give them a hot water bottle. Do not give them anything to eat or drink. Keep checking their breathing and pulse. If the person loses consciousness, be prepared to begin CPR if necessary (see pages 203–5).

SPLINTS, SLINGS AND THE TREATMENT OF BREAKS AND OTHER JOINT INJURIES

Fractures

There are two types of broken bone: open fractures and closed fractures. In an open fracture, the broken bone protrudes through the skin; in a closed fracture, it doesn't. First aid treatments for both types are similar, but with an open fracture you should cover the wound to keep it clean (see pages 207–9). Open fractures are easy to diagnose because you can see the bone jutting out. Closed fractures are more difficult and can only be properly diagnosed with an X-ray.

Severe sprains and dislocated joints can be just as painful. Symptoms include tenderness to the touch, swelling, disfiguration and difficulty or pain in moving the injured part. If you're not sure whether a bone is broken, treat it as if it is. Better safe than sorry.

The underlying treatment for all fractures is the same. Sit or lie the patient down. Then immobilize the break by securing the joints above and below with your hands or bandages, and call for help. This will prevent any further injury until medical help arrives. Most injuries can be supported with slings and/or bandages, but for extra support you can use splints. These can be fashioned from any straight piece of wood or metal – a thin but sturdy branch will do the trick when you're in the field. Always pad the area between the splint and the skin with something soft. Here's how to treat the most common breaks.

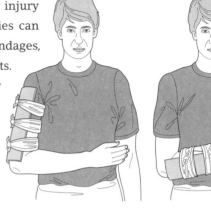

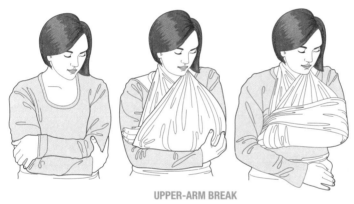

UPPER-ARM BREAK

Arm

There are two categories of arm break: upper and lower. The simplest method of immobilizing the arm and providing the necessary support for both kinds of break is by using a sling. To make a sling, you need a triangular piece of cloth (or a square one folded to make a triangle). Follow the procedure shown in the diagrams. For extra support, secure the arm by tying a broad bandage around the chest and over the sling; make sure that the broad-fold bandage is below the fracture site for an upper-arm injury. Once the sling is

LOWER-ARM BREAK

in place get help for the patient immediately.

If the break is more serious, however, you might want to support it with splints. Find two splints long enough to cover the joints above and below the fracture (the shoulder and elbow for an upper-arm break, the elbow and wrist for a lower-arm break). Fasten them in place with a piece of bandaging material or cloth at three locations – around the site of the break, near the joint above the break and near the joint below the break.

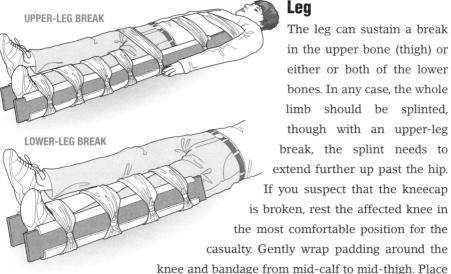

UPPER-LEG BREAK

LOWER-LEG BREAK

Leg

The leg can sustain a break in the upper bone (thigh) or either or both of the lower bones. In any case, the whole limb should be splinted, though with an upper-leg break, the splint needs to extend further up past the hip. If you suspect that the kneecap is broken, rest the affected knee in the most comfortable position for the casualty. Gently wrap padding around the knee and bandage from mid-calf to mid-thigh. Place a soft support such as a folded jacket underneath the knee for extra support and then add the splints as before. This injury is particularly painful so stop if it causes additional discomfort. Call for medical help.

Ribs

Without the benefit of an X-ray, it is very difficult to tell if someone has broken a rib. However, it's better to be safe than sorry. Symptoms of a broken rib include pain and difficulty in breathing. Sometimes the broken bone can puncture a lung, in which case the patient might cough up bright red, frothy blood.

An arm sling (see opposite) on the injured side will help immobilize the chest and prevent the injured rib from moving. If you suspect that the injury is serious then you can use an elevation sling (see page 214–5) for extra security. Alternatively, lie the patient down. Wrap at least one bandage round the chest so that it restricts the movement of the ribcage. Put something soft underneath and then tie the bandage(s) along the side of the ribcage opposite the break.

If the bandages cause discomfort, remove them. And if the ribcage appears depressed, don't apply any bandages at all.

Nose

A broken nose is quite easy to diagnose because the shape of the nose is often altered. However, the injured person should be assessed at a hospital, as there may also be other injuries to the head. The nose itself does not need to be splinted, but you can treat the other symptoms of a break. If there is bleeding from the nostrils, get the patient to sit down, hold their head up and breathe through their mouth. Squeeze the soft part of the nose just below the bone with your thumb and forefinger for about ten minutes and then gradually release the pressure. If the nose is still bleeding then pinch it for another ten minutes. If it is still bleeding after that then you will need to get medical help. If there is an exterior wound, apply direct pressure over a sterile dressing.

Jaw

Have someone with a jaw injury examined at a hospital as they might have sustained other head injuries. You can tell a broken jaw because the lower and upper jaws don't line up properly. Talking or swallowing will hurt the patient and there may be some bleeding around the gums. To alleviate pain and keep swelling down, apply a cold pad or an ice pack to the jaw.

Collarbone or shoulder

If a patient has broken their collarbone or dislocated their shoulder, they will naturally tend to hold their injured shoulder forward and down, with their elbow bent and their forearm across their chest, supported by the hand on their good side. You need to apply two triangular bandages to keep them

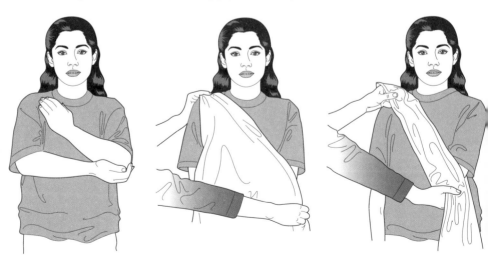

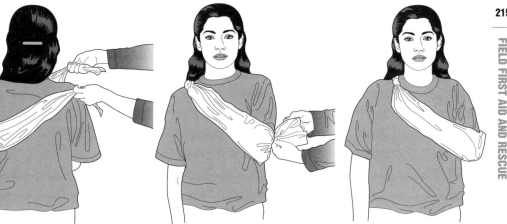

in this position. Fix one as an elevation sling (see diagrams above). Fold the second one in half lengthways twice to make it a broad bandage and wrap it around the arm and the chest so that it keeps the upper arm against the side of the body. Don't tie it so tight that it restricts the flow of blood.

Foot/toe

If a patient has a broken toe or foot, it can cause extremely rapid swelling. Get the shoe and sock off as quickly as possible – cutting them off with a knife if necessary. Elevate the injured foot and support it safely – this will supply some pain relief. Apply a cold pack. Wrap padding around it and bandage in place.

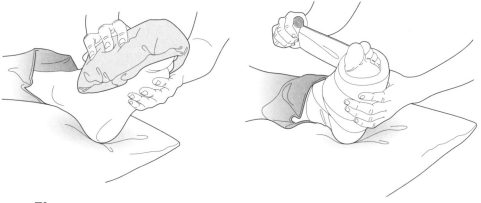

Finger

Remove any rings from the injured hand before the hand begins to swell. Immobilize the whole hand in padding and then put it in an elevation sling to help ease the pain.

Sprains

A sprain is an injury to the ligaments surrounding a joint. Ankles, fingers, wrists and knees are the most commonly affected. The symptoms are often similar to that of a closed fracture – if you're in any doubt as to whether you or your patient has a sprain or a fracture, you should treat it as the latter.

Sprains are normally a lot less serious than fractures. The best treatment is to apply ice to the injured area – but that can be in pretty short supply in the field! A sprained ankle, however, can be debilitating, so it's worth knowing how to treat it. Keep the patient's shoe on, but loosen the laces in case the injury causes swelling. The recommended treatment is **RICE**.

> **R** – **REST** the injury, so stop the person from walking.
>
> **I** – apply **ICE** if you can, but if you can't then you can cool the injury by soaking a towel in cold water and wrapping it around the wound.
>
> **C** – **COMFORTABLE** support and **COMPRESSION**. Apply a compression bandage that extends from the joint below the injury to the joint above it.
>
> **E** – **ELEVATE** and support the injury.

BURNS

As with all things medical, prevention is the best cure. In the field, there are plenty of opportunities for burning yourself. Never get complacent around fires and cooking implements and hopefully none of the following will apply to you.

Doctors divide burns into first- (superficial on the outer layer of skin), second- (intermediate) and third-degree (full-depth) categories, according to their severity. Superficial burns may be the most painful, deep burns may not hurt initially because nerves may be damaged. Treating burns in the field, however, remains the same for all categories.

- If possible, place the burn under cold running water to halt the burning process. Ten minutes or until the pain eases should do it. Call for medical help.

- If you don't have any running water, use any cold liquid.

- Remove any clothing, watches or jewellery from around the burnt area while you are cooling it and before it starts to swell; but don't remove anything that has stuck to the burn.

* If the skin has been damaged, the patient will experience fluid loss. In addition, all burns are susceptible to infection – even more so in the field. Cover the burn with a piece of cling film and cover a foot or hand with a plastic bag. If you don't have these, apply a sterile, non-fluffy dressing. Make sure nothing adhesive touches the damaged area – don't use plasters, as the burn may be larger than you think.

* Don't touch or try to pop any blisters – the skin is your body's natural defence against infection.

* There's an old wives' tale that says you should rub butter or lard on to a burn. This is a very bad idea – it'll only make things worse.

* Severe burns can cause shock. Look out for the symptoms and treat the casualty accordingly (see page 210–11).

Any burns on a child and any deep burns, even if they are small, should be looked at by a doctor as soon as possible.

ENVIRONMENTAL INJURIES – TREATING EXTREMES OF HOT AND COLD

Our body has evolved to control its core temperature very effectively, and there's a good reason for that. As we've already seen in Chapter 1, if our temperature dips below 28.8°C or goes above 42.7°C, we die; and if it strays just a little from its ideal temperature of 36.8°C, we can become very unwell.

Living in the wild, exposed to the elements, you are more than usually at risk from extremes of hot and cold. You need to know how to recognize and treat the symptoms of both.

IMPROVISING IN THE FIELD

A good field treatment for healing burns (but not for cooling them) is to soak a clean T-shirt in a boiling solution of tannic acid – tea – for ten minutes. Let the cloth cool and then wrap it around the burns. If you don't have any tea, you can make a tannic acid solution by boiling oak bark. This improvised field dressing is very effective for reducing the pain and speeding up the healing process. It also provides some protection against infection.

The effects of heat

Too much heat can have alarming consequences for us human beings. As usual, prevention is better than cure; so read Chapter 1 for the lowdown on what sort of gear you should be wearing to help the absorption and evaporation of sweat. Remember: layers are the key. They can be quickly and easily removed if you feel yourself getting too hot. Too much sun can cause heat exhaustion and even heatstroke.

Heat exhaustion is quite common; symptoms include dizziness, confusion, headaches, loss of appetite, nausea and sweating. If anyone is suffering from

Heatstroke can kill you – remember that prevention is better than cure.

IMPROVISING IN THE FIELD

It's very important to keep your head protected when you're in direct sunlight. If you don't have a hat, any article of clothing will do. In an emergency you can even make improvised headgear from foliage.

this, sit them down in the shade and get them to drink water, preferably containing rehydration salts.

Heatstroke – or sunstroke – occurs when our temperature increases and our bodies' cooling mechanisms become ineffective. Symptoms include headaches, drowsiness and strange behaviour. In extreme cases the patient may lose consciousness or even have seizures. Their skin is often very hot and dry to touch. Their pulse rate generally increases.

Many people dismiss the threat of heatstroke, but it can be very severe – sometimes fatal – and escalates very rapidly. It is generally brought on by vigorous exercise in hot conditions without sufficient rest or intake of water. If the weather is particularly hot, force yourself to drink a pint of water an hour and, if you're trekking, take regular rests in the shade. I have seen heatstroke strike both soldiers and camera crews. In the Sahara, three of our *Born Survivor* crew (of which there are only five in total!) were struck down by heatstroke and had to be evacuated as casualties. Once someone starts to go down, it happens very quickly, and it can take days of rehydration to recover fully. In the case of heatstroke, prevention really is better than cure.

Be aware that heatstroke is most common in hot, humid conditions. If the air is dry, sweat evaporates easily from the skin; when the air is humid, evaporation is more difficult, which means that the sweating mechanism is compromised and the body continues to heat up. If you do recognize the symptoms of heatstroke coming on, treatment is as follows:

- Stop moving.

- Get into the shade.

- If possible, the patient should be wrapped in a cold, wet sheet. You can keep the sheet wet by pouring cold water over it at intervals.

- Failing that, a damp cloth or an improvised fan will help bring their body temperature down. However, do not let the casualty get too cold.

BEAR'S SECRET SCOUTING TIPS

If the air is not too humid, you can cool your body down considerably by soaking your clothes in water. As the water evaporates it will lower your temperature.

▪ Extreme heatstroke can cause unconsciousness. Breathing may stop so be prepared to give CPR (see pages 203–5).

▪ Even if the symptoms of heatstroke have gone away, the patient should be closely monitored for a few days – they can quickly return. Restart cooling if their temperature rises.

Exercising in the heat can also cause salt loss. So be aware of this and add salt to your diet in conditions where you are sweating a lot (see page 95). Excessive sweating can also drain your body of vitamin C so, if possible, eating citrus fruits is a good idea.

The effects of cold

See Chapter 1 for everything you need to know about insulating yourself against the cold. When the ambient temperature drops, you need to increase your body's heat production while minimizing its heat loss. Eat plenty of food (see page 92) and keep moving so that your body produces natural heat. A top tip for cold hands is to swing your arms around vigorously for ten seconds. This forces blood into your cold extremities, instantly warming your fingers again. It works a treat! Make sure your clothing is loose (to keep your circulation going) and in layers. If necessary, take shelter. Remember to control your sweating – if your clothes become wet from inside, your body temperature will drop. If keeping warm is difficult, make sure as much of your skin is covered as possible: the smallest bare area is enough to make your core temperature plummet.

Hypothermia

If your body temperature dips just a few degrees, hypothermia becomes an imminent problem. It's principally thought of as a risk in high mountains and other cold regions; but you also need to be very aware of the symptoms of hypothermia when you get wet, especially if wind chill is a factor. Cold, wet, windy places are undoubtedly more dangerous than much colder, drier places, as people are often less well prepared and less suspecting of the power and danger of the elements. Remember the dangerous effects of wind chill (pages 165–6). Hypothermia is even more of a risk when you're exhausted, hungry or injured. Oh, and smaller people are more at risk than bigger ones!

It's easier to recognize the symptoms of hypothermia in yourself than in others: you'll find yourself shivering uncontrollably, becoming uncoordinated and making simple mistakes. Symptoms you will see in other people include shivering, quietness, slowness and a lack of coordination. (The Inuit have a good technique for assessing the effects of the cold. While they are ice fishing with their gloves off, they will touch their thumbs and little fingers together every few minutes. When this simple action becomes awkward and uncoordinated, they know it is time to rewarm their hands with their mittens.)

As hypothermia gets worse, the shivering will stop and the muscles will become stiff. The pulse might become irregular and the skin will be icy to the touch. Eventually, if left untreated, a person will become unconscious. If you suspect hypothermia in yourself or others, there are certain dos and don'ts.

Do:

- Take off any wet clothes and replace with dry ones – but only if there are spare ones. Never give a casualty your clothes.

- Insulate the body and head as much as possible. (I have used dry grasses stuffed in my clothing before.)

- Call for help – ideally send two people. Stay with the casualty.

- Rewarm the patient gradually. Give them lots of hot, sweet drinks; but no alcohol – it decreases the body's ability to retain heat as the blood races to the stomach and away from your extremities (so tots of whiskey are out!).

- Give the patient food high in carbohydrates and fat to provide energy.

Don't:

- Immerse the patient in very hot water. This can take any warm blood to the surface of the skin, away from where it is needed, and can take cold blood to the heart and brain, causing complications.

- Warm the arms and legs with direct heat. This can force cold blood back to the major organs and make things worse. It can also potentially cause burns, as the patient might not have good feeling in the cold limb. I have seen this happen before with soldiers warming their cold hands over a fire.

- Rub or massage the patient.

HIDDEN DANGERS

You should never rewarm a frostbitten area if there's a chance it will refreeze, as this can damage the flesh beyond repair. In an extreme survival situation, it's better to let the frostbite remain until help arrives. Hopefully that's something you'll never have to do.

If the patient loses consciousness, monitor their breathing and pulse rate carefully. Be prepared to give cardiopulmonary resuscitation (see pages 203–5) if necessary.

Frostbite

Frostbite occurs when your flesh freezes. The skin will go white and waxy, then red and swollen and eventually black. If it reaches the black stage, the likelihood is that the frostbitten area will have to be amputated. Mild frostbite, however, is reversible by *slowly* rewarming the area. This should be done in warm – not

hot – water; if there's none available, the patient should be wrapped in a blanket or sleeping bag so that their body heat can rewarm the affected part. You'll know it's 'done' when the area becomes swollen and red. Never rewarm over direct heat – the lack of sensation in the affected part may cause the patient to burn themselves. Don't rub the frostbitten area.

Be warned: rewarming frostbite is excruciatingly painful; offer the patient some pain relief such as paracetamol.

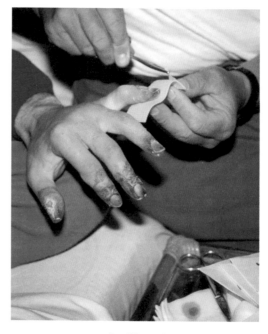

Frostbite can be excruciatingly painful and can result in the loss of limbs.

TRAVELLERS' AILMENTS

There are a number of illnesses you might encounter when you're in the field. Although many of these are not often encountered in our home countries, you should be aware of them if you're trekking in the more remote parts of the world. With a bit of luck, you'll be able to avoid most of them, but if you're travelling to an unfamiliar region, make sure you check with your doctor which diseases you will most be at risk from and make sure you get any vaccines or preventative medicines available. And if you suspect that any of your party is suffering from one of these illnesses in the field, evacuate them and get them to a doctor as quickly as possible.

Diarrhoea

Danger zones: Anywhere

What is it? A twofold or more increase in the number of unformed bowel movements

Transmission: Infected food or water

Symptoms: You know when you have it! But the medical definition is three or more loose stools per day.

Prevention: Be careful what you eat. In an area where diarrhoea is prevalent, avoid uncooked food and tap water (including ice). Imodium and Pepto-Bismol will help in most cases.

Cholera

Danger zones: Indonesia, much of Asia, Eastern Europe, and Africa

What is it? A bacterial disease of the intestine

Transmission: Passed in the stools and spread by contaminated food or water

Symptoms: Diarrhoea and/or vomiting – these both cause dehydration

Prevention: Vaccination gives some protection but is only 50 per cent effective. Avoid uncooked food and unbottled water.

Hepatitis A

Danger zones: Developing countries in Africa, Latin America, India and Mexico

What is it? A viral infection of the liver

Transmission: Food, water, contact with an infected person

Symptoms: Anything between a week and several months of fever, anorexia, nausea and abdominal pain, followed by jaundice

Prevention: Vaccination

Hepatitis B

Danger zones: Africa, India, the Middle East, some Pacific islands, Southeast Asia
What is it? An infection of the liver that can cause extensive liver damage, cirrhosis of the liver and liver cancer
Transmission: Blood, body fluids, needles
Symptoms: Fever, loss of appetite, nausea and abdominal pain, followed by jaundice
Prevention: Vaccination

Japanese encephalitis

Danger zones: Agricultural regions of Southeast Asia and the Far East
What is it? A viral disease that affects the central nervous system
Transmission: Mosquito bites
Symptoms: Range from being non-existent to severe and flu-like, with fever, chills, tiredness, headache, nausea and vomiting
Prevention: Vaccination

Malaria

Danger zones: More than 100 countries, including sub-Saharan Africa, India, Central and South America, Southeast Asia, the Middle East and Oceania. More than 40 per cent of the world's population is at risk from malaria.
What is it? An infectious disease caused by a parasite

Transmission: Mosquito bites
Symptoms: Fever and flu-like symptoms, including shaking, chills, headache, muscle aches and tiredness
Prevention: There are a number of malaria drugs available. Which one you take depends on where you are going (because some strains of malaria are resistant to certain drugs) and the side effects such drugs give you.

Bacterial meningitis

Danger zones: Mostly sub-Saharan Africa
What is it? A bacterial disease of the bloodstream or the meninges (a thin lining covering the brain and spinal cord). The same bacteria causes septicaemia, which often accompanies meningitis.
Transmission: Direct contact with the nose or throat discharges of an infected person
Symptoms: Fever, headache, nausea, vomiting, stiff neck, often a purple rash with pink skin discolorations
Prevention: Vaccination for some strains. Antibiotics may be given to anyone who has had close contact with a person who has meningitis.

Tetanus

Danger zones: Anywhere
What is it? A bacterial disease that affects the nervous system. Also called lockjaw.

Transmission: Via wounds contaminated with the organism which is found in soil, especially if it contains manure

Symptoms: Stiffness of the jaw, followed by stiffness of the neck, difficulty in swallowing, rigidity of abdominal muscles, spasms, sweating and fever

Prevention: Vaccination. You will have life-long immunity if you have received five doses of the vaccine in your lifetime.

Typhoid

Danger zones: Indian subcontinent, poor areas of Asia, Africa, Central and South America

What is it? A bacterial infection of the intestinal tract and sometimes the bloodstream

Transmission: Passed in the stools and spread by contaminated food or water

Symptoms: Sudden and sustained fever, headache, nausea, loss of appetite. Sometimes accompanied by a hoarse cough, constipation or diarrhoea.

Prevention: Vaccination. Avoid fruit or vegetables washed in local water, ice, ice cream from street vendors and unbottled water.

Yellow fever

Danger zones: Sub-Saharan Africa, tropical South America

What is it? A viral disease

Transmission: Mosquito bites

Symptoms: Fever, headache, vomiting and backache. As the disease progresses the pulse slows down and weakens, the gums bleed and blood appears in the urine. There may be jaundice.

Prevention: Vaccination

MIND, BODY, SPIRIT TO SURVIVE

health, fitness and eating right

To be a top Scout, it is vital that we learn to look after our bodies like a mechanic looks after a racing car. Keeping yourself fit, strong and healthy is a vital part of a Scout's job, or anyone living in the field. To achieve this, a lot comes down to how you eat and how you train. Good health and fitness allow us to act and think better, longer and faster. Scouts are trained to outwit, outrun and outperform normal people, and these skills come largely from eating right and training smart.

I am going to give you a summary of what I have learnt – mainly the hard way through trial and error, but also through masses of research and good fortune – on the subjects of health, nutrition and physical conditioning.

After I left the army I put on about 3 stone in weight. I smoked, I drank, I stopped training and I ate badly. I am not proud of this, but I guess in my case it was a reaction to all my years of hard physical work in the military. I wanted out and I got out... but I looked and felt awful! Then, one day, I decided to change. I decided that life was not going to pass me by. I wanted to grab the opportunities I had and not squander this precious gift of life and adventure. I stopped smoking and boozing. I started to run and train, and I educated myself about how to eat smart. This is what I have come away with, and it has worked well for me. Take from it what you will.

And by the way, the chances are that if you're going to follow the advice in this chapter, you'll need to change your lifestyle a bit. Change is never easy. It takes hard work and discipline. But if it *was* easy, everyone would be a Scout or climb Everest. Remember: easy doesn't achieve anything.

NUTRITION

Rule number one: if you feed your machine well, and feed it clean fuel, it will perform for you. Training hard but eating rubbish is a waste of time. In decades gone by, many athletes used to ignore nutrition in the belief that their health and performance were mainly down to how well they trained. Nutrition was a small addition to this. Now we know better, and it is well understood that a significant part of an athlete's performance is down to how he or she eats – even more so than how they train. If you are to perform at your peak, the most important thing you can do is to eat right.

In the main, I endeavour to have a diet based mainly on wholefoods. This means natural foods, as they are found in nature. Potatoes, fruits and vegetables

are found in nature, as are brown rice, lentils, pulses, spices, soya, nuts, avocados, honey, lentils, beans, quinoa, oats and natural chocolate to name a few. Doughnuts, white flour, white pasta, processed foods and biscuits are not! I try to avoid, as much as I can, too much animal produce, including dairy products like milk and cheese, as well as eggs and meat. I have fish in moderation. I also try to avoid white sugar, white bread, deep-fried foods, packets of crisps and processed or junk food. They are real baddies!

There is one other baddie that many people are unaware of and that is a type of 'manufactured' fat called trans-fat. This is the fat that makes doughnuts glisten nicely on a shelf for weeks on end. It is found in thousands of processed foods, from sweets and biscuits to ready meals. Trans-fat is seriously nasty. It is produced artificially in a process called hydrogenation, which turns liquid oil into solid fat. It is used because it is cheap, adds bulk to products, has a neutral flavour and gives products a long shelf life. But it is so bad for you and has such strong links to high cholesterol, that countries like Denmark and Switzerland – often pioneers in health and environmental issues – have almost completely banned it. It not only raises cholesterol, it also strips the body of any good cholesterol you have. Most shocking of all, the body is completely unable to break down trans-fatty acids, causing the fat to build up in the body, much like bacon grease clogging the kitchen pipes. Absolutely nothing rivals trans-fat in its ability to clog up the vital arteries leading into the heart and brain, so avoid it at all costs!

Remember the difference between good fat and bad fat (see pages 92–4)? Saturated fat comes from meat and fried food; trans-fat comes from processed food; good fat comes naturally from such things as nuts, avocados and flax seed. (If you want a serious super-food, add flax seed to your oats or smoothie. It lowers blood pressure and cholesterol, protects your bones and helps prevent cancer, diabetes and heart disease.) It is very easy to substitute milk and butter for oat milk (made from pressed oats) or soya milk and soya margarine. It is very easy to make a delicious apple crumble using oats and honey rather than white flour or white sugar. It's a simple choice to make – after all, one version does you good and the other does you bad. It is mainly a question of retraining yourself to think healthy and improvise. Ask yourself if what you are eating is clean, whole, natural food, or is it empty calories that give you nothing but sluggishness, pale skin and a spare tyre?

I aim to eat five smaller meals a day rather than a big meal once or twice a day. If you eat infrequently – less than every four hours – your metabolism slows to a crawl. Your body believes it is going into starvation mode, so it starts to 'store' food as fat. Our bodies have evolved over millennia to survive and, due to the infrequency of hunter-gatherer meals, to store away reserves if not fed properly. But we no longer lack food. Our culture's problem is the opposite. For most of us, food is readily available and therefore we often eat to excess. This excessive but irregular eating is an unhealthy combination.

One of the keys to keeping trim is to develop a fast metabolism that burns up calories very quickly. A fast metabolism isn't just genetic; you can build it through physical training and regular, healthy eating. If you don't eat regularly, your body looks elsewhere for energy. The easiest place for it to draw energy from is not from fat deposits, as people commonly think, but from your muscles. So, not eating regularly does not make you slim – it makes you fat and costs you valuable muscle! To lose fat you have to fire up your natural metabolism, train hard and reduce your overall calorific input slightly. So I try to eat at least every four hours, even if it's just an apple and a handful of unsalted nuts. Keep the metabolism fire burning and don't force your body to start burning its own fuel – your muscle.

Once you start to eat more like this – regularly and with less animal and processed produce – you will notice you have more energy throughout the day, without the traditional post-lunch dip in energy that people often experience. Our Western palates are swamped from birth by fat, sugar and salt. Once you rein these right back you will find you start to taste foods properly, and foods such as berries will 'explode' on your tongue rather than go unnoticed. The combinations of delicious meals you can make with wholefoods is vast. It just takes some bold experimenting and a willingness to educate yourself in healthy living.

A typical day for me will start with a decent breakfast. Research shows that if you have a good wholesome breakfast, you not only eat less during the rest of the day, you also keep your metabolism fired up. I almost always have a bowl of oats, with flax seed, oat milk, honey and a banana. Or I make a smoothie out of all of this blended together. Then, mid-morning and mid-afternoon, I have a snack of a handful of unsalted nuts, some fruit or, if I am hungrier, then a piece of wholemeal toast with honey, natural peanut butter (not the trans-fat kind!) or half an avocado. For lunch I might make a wholemeal bread sandwich with hummus (a great food to have regularly), rocket salad, avocado and tomato, followed by some fruit or a soya yogurt. For supper I try not to eat too late and might have baked sweet potato, or quinoa pasta, with a yummy veggie sauce and a salad. For pudding I might have a healthy crumble of fruit with oat topping (I love crumbles!).

Of course, there are many amazing combinations of great foods you can eat that not only taste good, but are also super-healthy. Look on the Internet for 'raw food cooking' or 'vegan recipes'. I am not saying that you should become a vegan or a raw-food-only person, but both camps have masses of unbelievably healthy, delicious recipes to offer the healthy-eating Scout. So get online and try some!

The one thing I would add to all this is to say that it's OK every now and again to have moments of 'weakness'! Good health is about how we eat and train for the majority of the time. Remember the 80/20 rule – if you eat clean, healthy wholefoods for 80 per cent of the time, it's all right to have a few treats for the remaining 20 per cent. There's a time to train and a time to have fun – or, as an old Royal Marine friend of mine used to say, work hard, play hard. The odd roast dinner or steak is great, as is a chocolate bar when you really crave one. And sometimes in the field it is just not possible to eat perfectly. When you are on a mission and you need calories. But do develop a good instinct about your nutrition, fitness and health. And when you are eating less healthy food out of choice or out of necessity, do your best to have some healthy food with it. Grab a handful of unsalted nuts and raisins before you tuck into a meat barbecue, or have some fruit with your chocolate bar.

Supplements

In general, I am not a believer in taking lots of synthetic vitamin supplements. More and more research shows that the body often struggles to absorb these unnatural vitamins efficiently and that a good diet, based on fruit, vegetables and starchy foods, combined with a good lifestyle, is the best way to improve and maintain our health over time.

The World Health Organization reminds us that we could stay healthier for longer if we took more care of our nutrition, following a diet mainly based on fruits, vegetables and starchy foods. They have therefore recommended, as part of their dietary advice, five portions of fruits and vegetables, preferably local, every day. Unfortunately many of us do not consume enough fruit and vegetables, and certainly not every day. The average consumption across Europe is less than half the recommended intake.

The only supplement I would recommend without reservation is a wholefood-based supplement called Juice Plus. I have used this since I was a teenager. It is an easy way to add good nutrition to your diet and involves taking a couple of fruit capsules in the morning and a couple of veg ones in the evening with a good-sized glass of water. It is the one supplement I always take with me on my expeditions, whether I'm climbing Everest or trekking through the filthiest jungles. What I like about Juice Plus is that the research behind it is so strong. It is one hundred per cent natural and provides raw, anti-oxidant fruit and veg in capsule form. For me it fulfils a key part of my nutrition, training and recovery needs. So I recommend you read about it and research it yourself, then get using it!

And finally, don't worry about not getting enough calcium or vitamins and minerals if you drop dairy products and meat from your diet. If you replace them with more fruit and veg then you will be fine. Vegetables like broccoli, for example, give you more than enough calcium. Remember: Americans drink more milk per head than almost any other nation in the world and still have huge problems with osteoporosis and other bone conditions. Excessive protein, such as that found in milk, actually strips the body of calcium as the kidneys work to excrete the excess. So stick to whole, natural, plant-based foods and your health and immune system will be strong and your body fuelled for adventure!

FITNESS

I always aim to train five or six days a week in a mix of different disciplines. This mainly involves alternating cross-country runs, strength training and yoga. These are the three types of exercise that give me a good, all-round fitness based on cardiovascular fitness, strength and flexibility. All three are vital to all-round fitness: it's no good being a muscle-bound meathead if you can't run, climb or touch your toes; likewise you are limited if you can run for miles but don't have the strength to climb a tree or carry a pack. I treat these three disciplines as the building blocks that allow me to do all the other sports I love, such as martial arts, gymnastics, acrobatics – and, of course, climbing, skydiving and paragliding.

On top of this I always make sure I get enough rest. Rest is a vital and often ignored part of training. The actual training itself is there to shock the muscles, to 'damage' them and put them under pressure, which then stimulates them to grow back and recover stronger. But that 'recover stronger' part happens when

TRAINING EXERCISES

Warming up before you exercise is an important part of all physical training. It is also a key part of ensuring you stay injury-free. So take a few minutes either to jog gently or skip, as well as including a bit of stretching and gentle strength training such as doing twenty half press-ups on your knees. It just tells your body to get pumping, get set and get ready for action!

you rest. So, without rest, you will limit your fitness. I aim for between seven and eight hours' sleep a night (not always easy with three young boys, mind!) and also to have at least one day a week free from exercise.

Let me break the disciplines down for you and describe *how* I train. You will no doubt adapt this regime to fit your own style and then make it your own, but this will provide you with a good basic framework. Remember that it is important not to over-train. This can hinder your progress and can also result in injury. Balance, as with so much in life, is one of the keys to good long-term fitness.

| Running

Bruce Lee called running the king of all exercises, and he was no slouch! In the French Foreign Legion they refer to running as their religion. It forms a great base for a lot of good fitness. The main aim of running is to increase your heart rate to a level where, like any muscle, it works hard and then, in your recovery and rest time, it strengthens.

Imagine a stream. When the water is stagnant and sits around hardly flowing, then it is dirty, old and smelly! When the stream is fast flowing the water is clean, crisp, dynamic and fast. Our bodies, cells and arteries are the same. When we don't use them, like a ship in a harbour, they rot. When the heart is working and blood is flowing around our muscles and cells, our bodies are like the fast-flowing stream. Pumping blood around our bodies cleans out all the bad toxins – car fumes, dust mites, etc. – that we accumulate as a result of day-to-day living. Pumping blood efficiently and breathing hard in the good, fresh, outdoor air both act to cleanse our bodies from the inside. Running makes all this happen.

Try and run outdoors if you can; it's better for you, you are in fresh air and it's less boring, which will enable you to run further. It will also improve your balance, as you have to adapt to the changing terrain on which you are running. I aim to run at a good pace about two or three times a week for between 30 and

*Running is the religion of the French Foreign Legion. It helps the
blood circulate freely and cleanses the body from the inside ...*

235

MIND, BODY, SPIRIT TO SURVIVE

40 minutes. This seems to be about the optimum running time. Much longer
and you risk injury; any less and you are not keeping the heart rate up for a
sustained enough period to stimulate muscle rebuilding and growth.

Running in such a way that our heart rate varies during the course of a jog is
the best way to increase fitness. So if you have hills around you, use them! Short
bursts up hills or short sprints interspersed along your route will increase the
benefits you get from your workout. What I call 'stretching' your heart and lungs
(as you do when you are breathing very hard up a hill) will stimulate greater
growth and recovery.

Sometimes (mainly when it is wet and cold and windy!) it is hard to find the
motivation to get outside and run. I have a simple rule for these moments: I will
commit to run for five minutes then, if I still don't feel like it, I will stop. What
invariably happens is that once I'm out there, moving around and warming
up, I come alive and love it! I run a lot on hills – working hard for some parts
then coasting a bit for others – to vary my heart rate. Above all I make sure my
exercise is enjoyable and therefore sustainable. If every run makes you vomit
with fatigue (as they often did in the military!) it kind of puts you off. Sometimes
I run hard, sometimes less so, but the main thing is that I am out there doing
myself some good.

With exercise, it is better to develop habits that last a lifetime than fads that last a week. So be your own judge, but keep it fun and sustainable. If you prefer aerobics in a studio or swimming in the local pool to running then fine. But do a good cardiovascular exercise, one that keeps the heart rate up there, at least two or three times a week.

I consider this time out running, with my dog, in the hills, to be my healing time. Time alone, time to be, time to think, to work hard, to sweat, to train and to find myself again among all the business of life. It might sound a bit wacky, but it works for me. It should work for you too. Good old Bruce Lee, eh?

Strength training

Strength is vital for almost every task a Scout will undertake. The stronger you are, the easier those tasks will be! But there is a big difference between flashy, big muscles and strong, efficient muscles. Muscles are there to serve your brain and your imagination, to enable you to perform difficult tasks. What you are after as a Scout is power when it is needed. Few of us are gifted with natural muscle definition and it takes time and discipline to build good core strength, but it is a vital part of health and fitness.

Working your muscles hard stimulates your metabolism, which in turn burns calories and keeps you lean and mean. When you run your metabolism drops back to its resting rate within an hour. But when you do strength training, your metabolism not only fires up more quickly, it also keeps burning at that higher rate for over 12 hours. So if you want to keep trim then the best exercise you can do is strength training.

Let's go through the principles of effective strength training.

Frequency, duration and style

Aim to do strength training three times a week. This will not only keep you strong, it also keeps your metabolism high, continually. So, if you are naturally skinny, you'd better get eating, buddy – and eating masses of that good wholefood, every few hours at least. You have some muscles that are about to need serious energy!

Variety in your regime is the key: keep mixing your training up, but always base it on the same sound principles. If, one week, you only train once or twice, or you even miss a whole week because you're on holiday, that's fine. There's no need to panic; your muscle strength won't start deteriorating that quickly. Like nutrition, it's all about what you do most of the time. So don't beat yourself up because you miss a training session, just get out there tomorrow and start afresh. Over time, however, try to make strength training part of your daily life. Even if you are out in the field, you don't need a gym to strength train; just improvise. I do workouts all over the world when travelling between Scout groups or filming. I improvise by training outdoors, hanging off tree branches, vaulting over fences or in the stairwell of a building! I don't want to make excuses to myself; I just want to keep focused and do the training. I consider it

There's never an excuse for not exercising –
and the key is improvisation.

Climbing is the ultimate all-body workout … and it's fun!

my own time, my chance to stay in shape, to stay sharp. It is now such a part of me that days without training feel somehow wrong. This is the key to fitness: it needs to become a daily habit, like eating or sleeping.

In many ways the best weight you have is your own body. There is no part of yourself you cannot train just by using your own weight and gravity. Improvise; challenge yourself and your buddies to think of cool exercises. See my lists on pages 241–7 and adapt them. Training with friends is the best way to push yourself and it's always fun. Choose an exercise, then challenge yourselves to reach a certain number of repetitions within a time limit.

As with running, I don't reckon you need to train for longer than 30–40 minutes. This is a good length of time in which to do your whole body, but it won't tire you out so much that you can't do anything for the rest of the day. It's also an easy amount of time to incorporate into your day. Do it first thing in the morning, in your lunch break or after work. You choose, but just do it! Although a lot of research has gone into trying to find out when is the best time to train, the fact is that it's different for everyone. What really matters is that you just train.

A good whole body workout – one I tend to use as a standard workout, which I can adapt, improvise and tweak as I feel is appropriate – follows on pages 241–7. Pick one exercise for each muscle group. Perform one set, take no more than a 30-second rest, then move on to the next muscle group until you have gone through all seven. At the end of that circuit of seven exercises, take a 2-minute rest, then repeat until you have done the whole circuit three times. It will take roughly 30 minutes.

Vary the number of repetitions you do, but a good range is 8–12 for each exercise until your muscles are exhausted and you can do no more. If you *can* do more than 12, increase the weight, slow the exercise down or get someone to hold you back gently. If you *can't* reach 8, reduce the weight or get someone to support you.

Core training

Core training means building a strong core, based around the middle of your torso. If your core stability and strength are good, you will be stronger for every exercise you do. Core training involves working your strong central muscles – not only your stomach muscles but also your side rotator and back muscles.

Aim to focus on good core strength and stability during every exercise. Maintain good posture – a straight back, soft knees and a balanced head position. If you use your core strength to perform exercises, you will be better balanced and stay injury-free. Most injuries come from a weak core, which results in over-compensation of a minor muscle, such as the lower back. For example, you might be doing bicep curls with a log. If it's too heavy, you will start bending and twisting in an attempt to lift it. By doing that you will have ceased to use your core strength and your body will be twisting out of position. This is likely to lead to injury. You would be much better off choosing a lighter log, which you can lift and lower steadily and slowly using your core strength.

The Scout who understands how to train and use his core strength will always be the strongest.

Variety

It is vital to mix up your training. If you have done two or three whole body circuits every week for a month, why not change to individual muscle routines for one week? Try six exercises for chest, six for shoulders and six for triceps on one day, then the same number for back, legs and biceps a couple of days later. Hammer them hard and shock them. Then maybe go back to a whole body circuit on the third workout of the week. One of the keys to strength training is to keep surprising your muscles. Muscles are very adaptable and quickly get to know what is expected of them. Very soon press-ups become easy, so force your chest to adapt to new things: put your feet on a log, or widen your grip, or explode very fast up, then go very slow down. I often get my kids to hold me round the waist for my pull-ups, or to sit on my shoulders for press-ups. It might mean I can only do a few reps, but it shocks my muscles and stimulates them to adapt and strengthen for the next time.

As I've already said, you should aim to work to exhaustion with each exercise; but you should also vary this. Maybe for the occasional workout keep it down to lighter weights and stop just before muscle fatigue. This type of variety is important if you want to gain strength.

Form over weight

It is more important to train correctly at a lower weight and for fewer repetitions than to break good posture or form. Keep good posture and position in your press-ups or pull-ups and they become much harder and much more effective.

Train slow, train fast

In other words, keep the actual movements during the strengthening exercises slow; aim for half of what feels a natural speed. Again, this isolates the muscles and puts them under much greater strain, as well as encouraging you to maintain form and posture. Then, in between exercises, train fast by keeping your rest time down to a minimum. This means that strength and circuit sessions also work your heart and lungs like a good cardiovascular session.

Keep switching the body parts you are exercising, so one individual body part doesn't become exhausted too soon. For example, don't simply do repeated press-ups with minimum breaks as your chest will tire before it has been properly exercised. Instead, move between press-ups, pull-ups, sit-ups and squats, with minimum resting time in between.

I am now going to give you a list of great body-part exercises and variations. You can pick and mix them to form your own workouts.

Legs

Squats

Squats use your core, back and shoulders as well as your legs. You can do these just with your hands on your head, nice and slow. You can widen your stance. Keep your back straight and sink your weight through your heels. Add weight across your shoulder, such as a branch – or a friend who wants a piggyback!

When you get good at these, try doing squats on one leg. Keep them shallow to start with, lowering just a little bit. Balance against something if you need to. Work up to full squats with no support – if you dare!

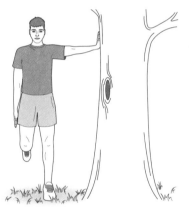

Calf raises

Stand with your toes on a step and your heels hanging over. Slowly rise up on to your toes, then down again. Add weight as you progress.

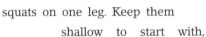

Chest

Press-ups

Perform these with your back straight. Slowly lower and raise your nose to and from the ground. Widen or narrow your hands to work different muscles. Get someone to push down gently on your shoulders as you perform these. Put your feet on a log or a chair. Focus on maintaining good core position. Try fast up, slow down. Try holding yourself in the down position for a minute!

Dips

With straight arms against your side, hold your weight between two well-balanced chair backs. Bend your arms to 'dip' your body between the chairs, then push hard up. Get two friends to hold the chairs in place if they are light!

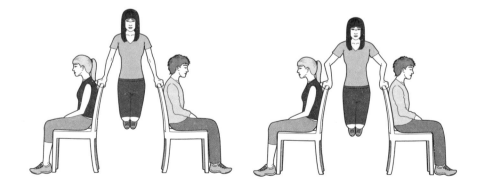

Isometric flys

Stand next to a tree with your arm straight out sideways and your palm towards the trunk. Squeeze intensively against the tree for a count of ten seconds. Switch arms. Holding exercises like these are known as isometrics and are great additions to your sessions.

Pull-overs

Lie on a bench on your back and with straight arms above your head and parallel to the ground. Now, lift a weight from that position until it is directly above your chest. The weight can be anything – just improvise.

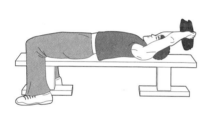 

Shoulders

Shoulder press

From standing, lift a weight steadily from shoulder level to full extension above your head. Go slow and steady. Try fast up, slow down. Try it balancing on one leg, engaging your core muscles. If you get good at these, try lowering yourself from a handstand position against a wall!

Shoulder flys

With a straight arm, lift a weight from your side to the horizontal. Try lifting it forward in front of you or,

with your body bent over at the waist, lift from the ground out to the side. From standing, raise your arms to the side and get a friend to push down gently on your hands. Hold for a count of ten. Try performing these exercises on one leg.

Back

Pull-ups

For this exercise you need a chinning bar above you, or the branch of a tree, or even a door frame. Grip it with your hands shoulder-width apart, with your palms facing away from you. Maintain a straight body position with no wobble.

Pull yourself up until your chin comes up to the bar (no neck reaching!). Go steady and get someone to help lift you from behind by the waist if you can't manage it unsupported. Build up gradually. Try a wide grip, a narrow grip and with your palms facing in. Lift your knees to your chest in between each rep. If you get really good, hold your legs out straight in front of you. Add weight around your waist if you need to, in order to keep your reps at around 8–12.

Bent-over row

Bend from the waist with a straight back and head up, then, with a wide grip, lift a log, bag or weight from the ground straight up towards your chest, then lower it again.

Triceps

Tricep extensions

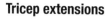

From standing, lift a weight above your head with both hands and slowly lower it behind your head, down the middle of your back.

Tricep dips

Sit with your back to a step and with your legs straight out in front of you. Put the palms of your hands flat on the step behind.

Push up until your arms are straight, then lower. Add weight to your lap as you need to.

Kick backs

Bend over at the waist, a weight in each hand. Keep your upper body and triceps parallel to the floor, then

force your fists back until your arms are straight. Try performing this exercise on one leg.

Biceps

The fact is that biceps are nothing more than poser muscles! To gain strength in them you must work your triceps in proportion. Biceps are a relatively small muscle group, so don't overwork them. Try to focus on working the major muscle groups: legs, chest, core and back.

Bicep curls

With a bag, log or weight in your hands, lift the weight to your chin. (You could also try lifting very light people from beneath their elbows with their elbows tucked in tight to their sides!) Don't sway or wobble. Keep your core strong and isolate the bicep muscles. Reduce the weight if needed. People often lift too much with bad posture and 'waste' the exercise. Try performing this exercise on one leg.

Core

Everyone wants a six-pack! But everyone *has* a six-pack... it's just that in most cases it's hidden beneath a load of fat! The best way to reveal it is to be lean, strong and fit. You can't just do masses of sit-ups and think you will get a six-pack. You can't burn fat from an individual muscle – when you exercise the body draws calories from all over. So eating smart is the key to a six-pack.

A strong core, lower back and stomach, as I have already emphasized, are the key to all strength. Exercise with good posture and good form and your core, stomach and lower back will automatically get strong. Here, however, are some good exercises specifically for those areas.

Dorsal raises

Lie on your front with your toes touching the ground and gently raise your upper torso off the ground a few inches. Don't jerk or over-extend your neck and head. Control it.

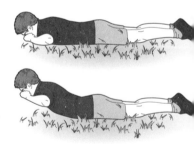

Flutter kicks

On your back, bring your knees to your chest then extend your legs away from you out straight so they are 30cm off the ground. Keep this position and then tap your heels together and apart. Alternatively, bring one knee into your chest then extend it again. Then repeat with the other knee.

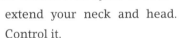

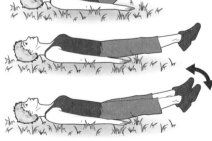

Pretend rope-climb

Lie on your back with your knees bent, your feet flat on the floor and your arms straight above you pointing to the sky. Pretend there is a rope dangling down to your chest. Reach out and climb up it. Move your arms up, down, keep climbing! This is hard work and a great core exercise.

Sit-up swaps

You need a friend with you to do this one. Sit down opposite each other, leaving enough space between you. Lie back with your knees bent. Sit up and pass a log to each other then go back down. Repeat. I love this one!

Side-bends

Stand with your legs shoulder-width apart, a small weight in one hand. Bend sideways from the waist to the side without the weight. Change sides.

Group training exercise

If you're in the field or with friends you could try this group exercise. Pick a muscle group, for example the chest, and one exercise, for example press-ups. Split up into two groups. One group does the exercise, the other is in charge of timekeeping. Start with one press-up and a ten-second rest, then two press-ups and a ten-second rest, then three. Keep increasing the number of press-ups and see how high you can get. Above 12 is very good! It sounds easy, but the numbers build very fast and the ten-second rest goes quickly. Add up the number of press-ups each member of the first group reached for a collective target that the second group has to beat. Each session will only last about fifteen minutes and you can pick a new exercise each day. The groups can change to keep it even, and everyone gets a fun workout. By the end of a week of these, you will all be super-strong!

FLEXIBILITY

Flexibility is the unsung hero in an athlete's arsenal. Most people neglect it, but do so at their peril. Being flexible is one of the keys to staying injury-free and keeping the joints moving fully and well.

For myself, I do at least one full yoga session every week, and I do it anywhere! Quietly tucked away in a corner of an airport, or on my own outside in the woods. I have always regarded it as a time to slow down, stretch out those muscles that have been worked well from the runs and circuits, and allow the blood to flow into the tight, restricted areas of our bodies that rarely tend to get reached. Of course, it's not just yoga that can do this – Pilates, gymnastics and simple stretching can all send blood pumping around our bodies. By doing this our blood can clean out all those hidden toxins. Don't forget to lie flat on your back, legs and arms extended, for at least five minutes and allow your body to do its cleansing work at the end of each session. Enjoy that quiet, still time. The toxins will then be flushed out through your pee, so remember to drink lots of water after each session. My body always tingles like mad and it is an amazing feeling – as if I am being given an internal de-frag!

As with running and strength training, everyone has a different preference, a routine they enjoy, and there are many different styles of exercise to get some flexibility into your body. It's horses for courses. I have found a simple yoga routine that lasts about 40 minutes and which I have followed and followed until I know it by heart. I also pick a few stretches to do in between my yoga sessions.

Keeping flexible is the best way of staying injury-free.

When I broke my back in a freefall accident many years ago, I had physio every week for years. Then I discovered that a good yoga session once a week did exactly the same thing. If anything, it was better. It freed my back up, kept it supple and stretched it. Most back injuries are the result of slipped discs, which are a direct result of a lack of mobility. So stretch your back and your body and keep it fluid and supple and when, as can easily happen when you're out hiking, you slip and twist an ankle or leg, you will be able to survive it without injury. That is a major motivation to do yoga – you don't hear about cats with twisted paws or slipped discs, because they are always stretching!

I'd recommend joining a yoga class to learn the ropes. Then you'll be able to follow a simple routine and adapt it for yourself. Again, aim for a session of about 30–40 minutes. Hold stretches for between ten seconds and a minute. Breathe through every stretch. Close your eyes. Breathe deeply into the stretch again. Relax. Let the mental and physical tensions slip away, breathe them away and stretch them away.

Remember to warm up before a stretching session, even if it is just a brisk walk. Work through each muscle group, from your head and neck to your ankles and feet. Work on your chest, shoulders, triceps, lower back, upper back, stomach, hips, bottom, quads, hamstrings and calves. Then enjoy the post-stretch healing tingle!

THE SPIRITUAL

I have learnt over the years, from numerous expeditions, close calls and hairy moments, that it takes a proud man to say that he never needs any help. And I have yet to meet an atheist in the Death Zone of Everest, or in a lifeboat!

Faith is always hard to write about. And if it is to be real and meaningful, it will also be very personal. But that is part of what makes believing so special. You might be a Christian, Muslim, a Hindu or a Buddhist... or you might be none of these. Ultimately, you must decide for yourself whether you are going to include a spiritual dimension to your life. For what it's worth, I can tell you that life becomes a lot wilder and a lot more fun if you do!

I guess the best way I can write this section is simply and intimately to say what my Christian faith means to me and how it has helped me time and time again. So here we go...

Living with faith will always brighten your day.

Life is a journey and at times we all need a guide. For me, that guide has become much more than simply a pointer of the way. He has become my backbone, my helper, my companion and my friend.

Jesus said, 'I have come so that you may have life, and have it in abundance.' That was a bit of an eye-opener for me. I always thought that Christianity was about being very sensible and acting all smart and religious. But the more I discovered about Jesus Christ himself, the more I found a man who was as unreligious as you can imagine. In fact, when he talked about finding faith and entering heaven he said, 'Unless you become like one of these [children], you will never enter the kingdom of heaven.' It seemed that the very heart of the Christian faith was not about church, pulpits, sermons or Latin verse! It was about a relationship with someone who promises us life in abundance, joy within, peace without and freedom in our soul. Now I was interested! And if that wasn't enough, he had a habit of turning water into wine to make a great party...

At the root of man's struggles is the fact that we are all flawed. Deep down in the pit of my soul, I know that I have messed up and done wrong, many times over. But Jesus said to those who knew their need for God, that the 'Son of Man had come to seek and save those that were lost'. Remember the story in the Bible of the woman who longed just to touch the hem of Jesus' cloak, knowing that in so doing she would be healed of her illness? Or the man who hung on a cross beside Jesus asking him to forgive him his many sins? They wanted what only He could give: freedom. Jesus' words were nectar to that man on the cross and they are nectar to me today – when we turn to Jesus, simply and honestly, and ask for forgiveness, we are made clean. When I first understood this, a wave of love flooded over me and healed so much pain. No wonder so many men and women through the ages have talked about the 'peace of God that passes all understanding'. Such love, such forgiveness, is beyond understanding and logic. But that is what makes the gift of God's love so special.

If we look back in time, there are not many great people or leaders who have not, quietly in their hearts, bent their knee and looked upwards to Jesus for help, strength, resolve and peace. Look at Isaac Newton, Christopher Columbus, the

Wright brothers, Joan of Arc, Richard the Lionheart, Abraham Lincoln, George Washington, Winston Churchill, Nelson Mandela, Galileo, Leonardo da Vinci and, of course, the Scouting founder, Baden-Powell. All were men and women of faith.

Faith is personal, so it is OK to use it personally. It is a gift for you, bought by Jesus at a great price. He died on a cross, tortured to death, in our place, so that we could be forgiven and set free. No wonder the overwhelming Christian emotion is gratitude. And when we live a life full of gratitude, that light spreads far and wide. We become calmer, nicer, friendlier; we laugh more, give more, we become more encouraging, more empowered, gentler, more fun and probably wilder. These fruits of the Spirit are a bi-product of a relationship with our Maker.

To me, the Christian faith is about finding home and finding our Father. I need both those things in my life, and I am not too proud to admit it. My Christian faith makes me stronger and it makes me smile. It is the secret power in my life. People ask me whether faith is a crutch. Well, what does a crutch do? It helps us stand. So in some ways I guess, yes, it is a crutch, but it is more than that to me. It's like a crutch that runs straight through my core. More like a backbone.

So if you have yet to find this sort of faith for yourself, be bold, take a step. What do you have to lose? What do you have to gain? Say a simple prayer in your head (don't worry, no one but God is listening!) and ask for Jesus to come into your life and stand beside you. Wonders will start to happen, I assure you.

I am going to give you one story and a few key verses to help you. Both have helped me through my own life. I hope they help you find home.

One night a man had a dream.
He dreamed he was walking along the beach with the Lord.
Across the sky flashed scenes from his life.
For each scene, he noticed two sets of footprints in the sand:
    one belonging to him, and the other to the Lord.
When the last scene of his life flashed before him
    he looked back, at the footprints in the sand.
He noticed that many times along the path of his life
    there was only one set of footprints.
He also noticed that it happened at the very lowest and saddest
    times of his life.
This really bothered him and he questioned the Lord about it:

'Lord, you said that once I decided to follow you,
    you'd walk with me all the way.
But I have noticed that during the most troublesome times in my life
    there is only one set of footprints.
I don't understand why when I needed you most you would leave me.'
The Lord replied:
'My son, my precious child, I love you and I would never leave you.
During your times of trial and suffering, when you see only one set of
    footprints, it was then that I carried you.'

I always carry the following verses from the Bible with me, hidden away:

'I will not be afraid for you are close beside me.' Psalm 23:4

'I can do all things through Christ who strengthens me.' Philippians 4:13

'The Lord himself watches over you.' Psalm 71:1–3

'Be strong and courageous for the Lord your God is with you.' Joshua 1:9

'Be sure of this, that I am with you, even to the ends of the world.'
    Matthew 28:20

'I am holding you by your right hand [...] do not be afraid; I am here to
    help you.' Isaiah 41:13

Now that is what I call life-enhancing!

MOTIVATION

This is the last part of the book, but in many ways it is the part that drives everything else. Without the motivation to get out there and make things happen, nothing ever does! It all comes from having a dream and then the determination to follow it. But what if I fail? What if it all goes wrong? Fear of failure is one of the biggest killers of adventure, imagination and dreams. The best advice I was given was that if you want to succeed, get out there and fail 22 times. The likelihood is that by the time you get to nine you will have hit the bullseye and succeeded anyway! So fail your way to success.

How will I raise the funds for my adventures? Stop making excuses. Get out there and start writing letters, knocking on doors, offering services in return for support. Just begin! That is often the hardest part. And remember this quote:

It is not the critic who counts: not the man who points out how the strong man stumbles or where the doer of deeds could have done better. The credit belongs to the man who is actually in the arena, whose face is marred by dust and sweat and blood, who strives valiantly [...] who, at the best, knows, in the end, the triumph of high achievement, and who, at the worst, if he fails, at least he fails while daring greatly, so that his place shall never be with those cold and timid souls who knew neither victory nor defeat.

Theodore Roosevelt

No one ever raised a statue to a critic. People who ridicule or put you down are often jealous, because even if you fail at least you had the balls to get out there, make a difference and live a bit, whereas the timid dare not.

I love the motto, 'Paddle your own canoe'. You shouldn't sit around complaining or making excuses about why you can't do something. You shouldn't assume it is someone else's job to make you happy or wealthy or adventurous. It says get out there and paddle! Forge your own path, be a leader, lead from the front. Remember the motto of the SAS: Who Dares Wins. The person who risks nothing, gains nothing.

So, now you have decided to go for it, how do you keep going? People say to me, 'But all this motivation is so temporary. It can never last.' Of course it's temporary... but so is washing! That's why you gotta keep doing it. You've got to keep putting the good stuff in and only then will you get the good stuff out. So, keep hanging out with like-minded people, people who value others, people who value adventure, people who value dreams. We become like those we hang out with, so choose your friends wisely and then help each other to keep charging.

But sometimes it gets so hard. Of course it does! But hard means there is an opportunity to keep going, to endure more than the others who quit. Hard provides you with a chance to shine. It is in the big moments of life that we learn who we really are. That is the time to come alive.

I wasn't the fittest soldier on SAS selection, but I was stubborn and kept going when it cut up rough. I wasn't the best karate guy when I started martial arts, but I kept going week after week, year after year. And I got my black belt. Worthwhile things take sacrifice and effort. That's what makes them special. Life doesn't reward the best or most talented. It rewards the dogged.

I want to finish this book with a simple phrase, one that sums up both adventure and Scouting. I love it. 'Life is really very simple: what we put in is what we get out.'